MW00653782

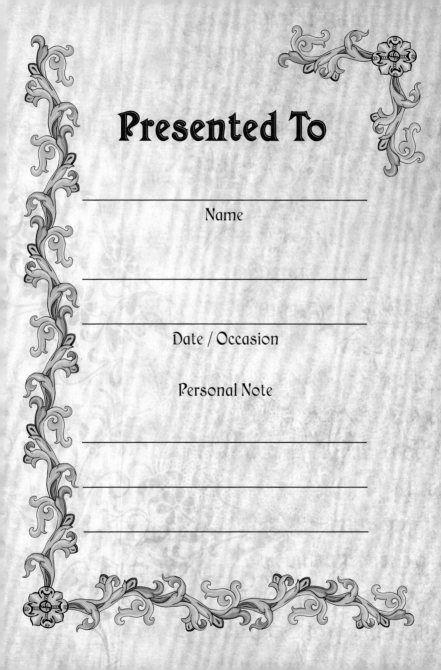

Presented To

_____

Name

_____

_____

Date / Occasion

Personal Note

_____

_____

_____

Behold Thy Mother

An English/Latin
Scriptural Rosary

Old and New Testament Passages

Imprimatur
Most Reverend Peter F. Christensen
Bishop of the Diocese of Boise

Deo
Gratias
Publications

ISBN 978-0-9972651-0-1
Copyright # TXu 2-019-205 © 2016
2 3 4 5 6 7 8 9 10

Deo Gratias Publications
25 Greenville Rd.
Alta, WY 83414
deogratiaspublications@gmail.com

All Scripture passages are based on the Douay Rheims Clementine
version and Latin Vulgate with selected inclusions from the
Revised Standard Version, Second Catholic Edition Bible.

Source of graphics used in this book:
Alfredo Malchiodi Graphic Arts Studio
www.alfredom.com

Printed in China
Shenzhen Kingfu Color Printing Co., Ltd.
(Thank you for all your help Bill Chou!)
www.kfprinter.com
bill@kfprinter.com

edicated to
Saint Joseph,
Chaste Guardian of
the Virgin.

In thanksgiving for the infinite love,
mercy, and generosity of God.

The people that walked in darkness have
seen a great light. Isaiah 9:2

Mary, Mother of the Church, this book is
published in your honor, and in reparation
for the offenses committed against
your Immaculate Heart.

The Rosary

he Rosary is the book of the blind, where souls see and there enact the greatest drama of love the world has ever known; it is the book of the simple, which initiates them into mysteries and knowledge more satisfying than the education of other men; it is the book of the aged, whose eyes close upon the shadow of this world, and open on the substance of the next. The power of the Rosary is beyond description.

—Venerable Archbishop Fulton Sheen (1895 - 1979)

Fruits of the Hail Mary

Just as the salvation of the world began with the *Hail Mary*, so the salvation of each individual is bound up with it. This prayer ... brought to a dry and barren world the *Fruit of Life*, and ... will cause the Word of God to take root in the soul and bring forth Jesus.

—St. Louis de Montfort (1673 - 1716)

mid this variety of languages a primary place must surely be given to that language which had its origins in *Latium*, and later proved so admirable a means for the spreading of Christianity throughout the West. And since in God's special Providence this language united so many nations together under the authority of the Roman Empire— and that for so many centuries— it also became the rightful language of the Apostolic See. Preserved for posterity, it proved to be a bond of unity for the Christian peoples of Europe.

Of its very nature Latin is most suitable for promoting every form of culture among peoples. It gives rise to no jealousies. It does not favor any one nation, but presents itself with equal impartiality to all and is equally acceptable to all.

Nor must we overlook the characteristic nobility of Latin formal structure. Its "concise, varied and harmonious style, full of majesty and dignity" makes for singular clarity and impressiveness of expression.

For these reasons the Apostolic See has always been at pains to preserve Latin, deeming it worthy of being used in the exercise of her teaching authority "as the splendid vesture of her heavenly doctrine and sacred laws." She further requires her sacred ministers to use it, for by so doing they are the better able, wherever they may be, to acquaint themselves with the mind of the Holy See on any matter, and communicate the more easily with Rome and with one another.

Thus the "knowledge and use of this language," so intimately bound up with the Church's life, "is important not so much on cultural or literary grounds, as for religious reasons." These are the words of Our Predecessor Pius XI, who conducted a scientific inquiry into this whole subject, and indicated three qualities of the Latin language which harmonize to a remarkable degree with the Church's nature. "For the Church, precisely because it embraces all nations and is destined to endure to the end of time ... of its very nature requires a language which is universal, immutable, and non-vernacular."

Since "every Church must assemble round the Roman Church," and since the Supreme Pontiffs have "true episcopal power, ordinary and immediate, over each and every Church and each and every Pastor, as well as over the faithful" of every rite and language, it seems particularly desirable that the instrument of mutual communication be uniform and universal, especially between the Apostolic See and the Churches which use the same Latin rite.

When, therefore, the Roman Pontiffs wish to instruct the Catholic world, or when the Congregations of the Roman Curia handle matters or draw up decrees which concern the whole body of the faithful, they invariably make use of Latin, for this is a maternal voice

acceptable to countless nations.

Furthermore, the Church's language must be not only universal but also immutable. Modern languages are liable to change, and no single one of them is superior to the others in authority. Thus if the truths of the Catholic Church were entrusted to an unspecified number of them, the meaning of these truths, varied as they are, would not be manifested to everyone with sufficient clarity and precision. There would, moreover, be no language which could serve as a common and constant norm by which to gauge the exact meaning of other renderings.

But Latin is indeed such a language. It is set and unchanging. It has long since ceased to be affected by those alterations in the meaning of words which are the normal result of daily, popular use. Certain Latin words, it is true, acquired new meanings as Christian teaching developed and needed to be explained and defended, but these new meanings have long since become accepted and firmly established.

Finally, the Catholic Church has a dignity far surpassing that of every merely human society,

for it was founded by Christ the Lord. It is altogether fitting, therefore, that the language it uses should be noble, majestic, and non-vernacular.

In addition, the Latin language "can be called truly catholic." It has been consecrated through constant use by the Apostolic See, the mother and teacher of all Churches, and must be esteemed "a treasure ... of incomparable worth." It is a general passport to the proper understanding of the Christian writers of antiquity and the documents of the Church's teaching. It is also a most effective bond, binding the Church of today with that of the past and of the future in wonderful continuity. ...

—Pope Saint John XXIII (1881 - 1963)
Apostolic Reign (1958 - 1963)

Illuminated Manuscripts

n illuminated manscript is a handwritten book in which the text is embellished with elaborately decorated, brilliantly colored, silver leaf and gilded images.

In the early Middle Ages, before the age of the university, monasteries were the central places of learning. Texts had to be laboriously copied by hand, as the printing press had yet to be invented. The monks of the time were the sole artisans of these exquisite works of art.

The majority of books were produced for use at Mass and for daily prayer (Books of Hours). The candlelight reflecting off the gilded pages "illuminated the text that it might be more easily read. The manuscripts were written on either vellum (calf skin) or parchment (sheep or goat skin). When the artwork was completed, the pages were handsewn together and bound with either leather or wood.

During a homily given by an English bishop to monk copyists in the twelfth century at Durham Cathedral, the bishop elaborated upon the great dignity accorded illuminated manuscripts and the materials used in their production.

"You write with the pen of memory on the parchment of pure conscience, scraped by the knife of Divine fear, smoothed by the pumice of heavenly desires, and whitened by the chalk of holy thoughts. The ruler is the Will of God. The split nib is the joint love of God and our neighbor. Coloured inks are heavenly grace. The exemplar is the life of Christ."

The invention of the printing press in the 1450's eventually phased out the production of these highly treasured works of art.

"Honor Thy Father and Thy Mother."

Exodus 20:12

Virgin and Child
William-Adolphe Bougereau (1825 - 1905)

"Behold Thy Mother."

John 19:27

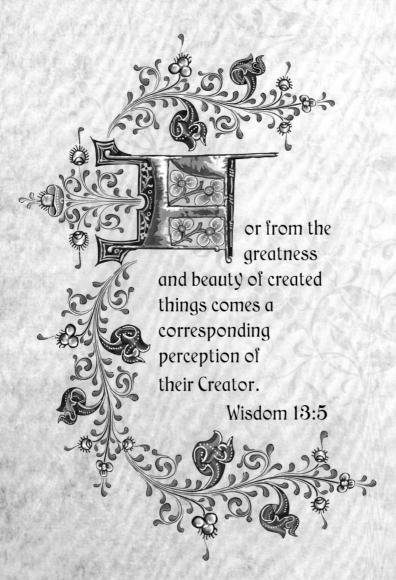

F or from the greatness and beauty of created things comes a corresponding perception of their Creator.

Wisdom 13:5

hatever is true,
whatever is honorable,
whatever is just,
whatever is pure,
whatever is lovely,
whatever is gracious,
if there is any excellence,
if there is anything worthy of praise,
think about these things.

Phillippians 4:8

We Stand on the Shoulders of Giants

We are like dwarves on the shoulders of giants, so that we can see more than they, and things at a greater distance, not by virtue of any sharpness of sight on our part, or any physical distinction, but because we are carried high and raised up by their giant size.

—Bernard De Chartres (d. 1130)

Table of Contents

Page

How to pray the Rosary 28

Prayers of the Rosary 31

Symbolum Apostolorum 32

The Apostles' Creed 33

Pater Noster 34

The Lord's Prayer (Our Father) 35

Ave Maria 36

Hail Mary 37

Gloria Patri 38

Glory Be 39

Oratio Fatimae 40

Fatima Prayer 41

	Page
Salve Regina	42
Hail, Holy Queen	43
Oratio quae dicatur post Rosarium	44
Concluding Prayer	45
Sancte Michael Archangele	46
Prayer to St. Michael	47
The Joyful Mysteries	49
The Sorrowful Mysteries	107
The Glorious Mysteries	163
The Luminous Mysteries	225
Index of Meditations	298
Index of Sacred Art	306

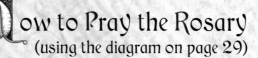

How to Pray the Rosary
(using the diagram on page 29)

1. Make the Sign of the Cross.

2. The Apostles' Creed. (See page 34 or 35 for the prayer).

3. The Lord's Prayer. (See page 36 or 37 for the prayer).

4. The Hail Mary. (See page 38 or 39 for the prayer).

5. The Glory Be. (See page 40 or 41 for the prayer).

6. The Fatima Prayer. (See page 42 or 43 for the prayer).

7. Announce the First Mystery.

8. Read the corresponding Scripture verse.

9. Announce the Second Mystery.

10. Announce the Third Mystery.

11. Announce the Fourth Mystery.

12. Announce the Fifth Mystery.

13. The Hail, Holy Queen. (See page 45 or 46 for the prayer).

14. The Concluding Prayer. (See page 46 or 47 for the prayer).

15. The Prayer to Saint Michael. (See page 48 or 49 for the prayer).

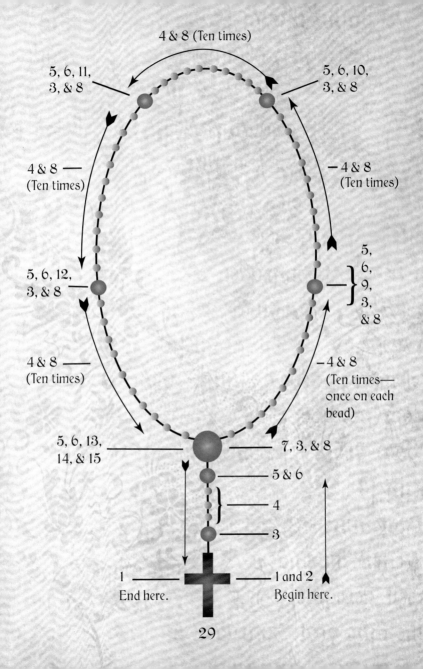

4 & 8 (Ten times)

5, 6, 11, 3, & 8

5, 6, 10, 3, & 8

4 & 8 —
(Ten times)

—4 & 8
(Ten times)

5, 6, 12, 3, & 8

5,
6,
9,
3,
& 8

4 & 8 —
(Ten times)

—4 & 8
(Ten times—
once on each
bead)

5, 6, 13, 14, & 15

7, 3, & 8

5 & 6

4

3

1
End here.

1 and 2
Begin here.

29

Traditionally, the various Mysteries are prayed on these days:

Joyful Mysteries: Monday and Saturday

Sorrowful Mysteries: Tuesday and Friday

Glorious Mysteries: Sunday and Wednesday

Luminous Mysteries: Thursday

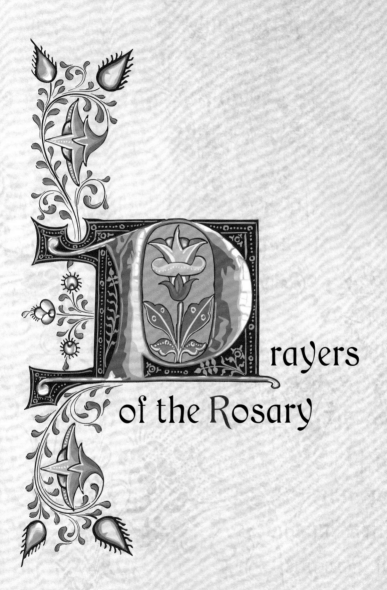

Prayers of the Rosary

Symbolum Apostolorum

Credo in Deum Patrem omnipotentem,
Creatorem caeli et terrae. Et in Jesum Christum
Filium eius unicum, Dominum nostrum, qui
conceptus est de Spiritu Sancto,
natus ex Maria Virgine,
passus sub Pontio Pilato, crucifixus,
mortuus, et sepultus, descendit ad inferos,
tertia die resurrexit a mortuis,
ascendit ad caelos, sedet ad dexteram
Dei Patris omnipotentis, inde
venturus est judicare vivos et
mortuos. Credo in Spiritum Sanctum,
sanctam Ecclesiam catholicam,
sanctorum communionem,
remissionem peccatorum,
carnis resurrectionem,
vitam aeternam.
Amen.

The Apostles' Creed

I believe in God, the Father Almighty, Creator of heaven and earth; and in Jesus Christ, His only Son, Our Lord, Who was conceived by the Holy Spirit, born of the Virgin Mary, suffered under Pontius Pilate, was crucified, died and was buried; He descended into hell; on the third day he rose again from the dead; He ascended into heaven and is seated at the right hand of God, the Father Almighty; from there He will come to judge the living and the dead. I believe in the Holy Spirit, the holy catholic Church, the communion of saints, the forgiveness of sins, the resurrection of the body, and life everlasting. Amen.

Pater Noster

Pater noster, qui es in caelis,
sanctificetur nomen tuum.
Adveniat regnum tuum.
Fiat voluntas tua, sicut in caelo et
in terra. Panem nostrum
quotidianum da nobis hodie, et
dimitte nobis debita nostra
sicut et nos dimittimus debitoribus nostris.
Et ne nos inducas in tentationem,
sed libera nos a malo.
Amen.

The Lord's Prayer
(Our Father)

Our Father, who art in heaven,
hallowed be Thy name;
Thy kingdom come;
Thy will be done on earth as it
is in heaven. Give us this day
our daily bread; and forgive us
our trespasses as we forgive
those who trespass against us;
and lead us not into temptation,
but deliver us from evil.
Amen.

Ave Maria

Ave Maria, gratia plena,
Dominus tecum.
Benedicta tu in mulieribus,
et benedictus fructus ventris tui,
Jesus.
Sancta Maria, Mater Dei,
ora pro nobis peccatoribus,
nunc, et in hora mortis nostrae.
Amen.

Hail Mary

Hail Mary, full of grace,
the Lord is with thee.
Blessed art thou among women,
and blessed is the fruit of thy womb,
Jesus.
Holy Mary, Mother of God,
pray for us sinners, now
and at the hour of our death.
Amen.

Gloria Patri

Gloria Patri, et Filio,
et Spiritui Sancto. Sicut erat
in principio, et nunc,
et semper, et in saecula
saeculorum.
Amen.

Glory Be

Glory be to the Father, and to the Son,
and to the Holy Spirit. As it was
in the beginning, is now, and
ever shall be. World
without end.
Amen.

Oratio Fatimae

O mi Jesu, dimitte nobis debita nostra,
libera nos ab igne inferni,
conduc in caelum omnes animas,
praesertim illas,
quae maxime indigent
misericordia Tua.

Fatima Prayer

O my Jesus, forgive us our sins,
save us from the fires of
hell. Lead all souls to
heaven, especially those
who are most in need
of Thy mercy.

Salve, Regina

Salve, Regina, Mater misericordiae.
Vita, dulcedo et spes nostra, salve.
Ad te clamamus, exsules filii Hevae.
Ad te suspiramus, gementes et flentes
in hac lacrimarum valle.
Eia ergo, advocata nostra,
illos tuos misericordes oculos ad nos converte.
Et Jesum, benedictum
fructum ventris tui, nobis
post hoc exsilium ostende.
O clemens, o pia,
o dulcis Virgo Maria.

V. Ora pro nobis, sancta Dei Genitrix.
R. Ut digni efficiamur promissionibus
Christi.

Hail, Holy Queen

Hail, holy Queen, Mother of mercy,
our life, our sweetness and our hope.
To thee do we cry, poor
banished children of Eve.
To thee do we send up our sighs,
mourning and weeping
in this valley of tears.
Turn, then, most gracious Advocate,
thine eyes of mercy toward us,
and after this our exile, show unto us
the blessed fruit of thy womb, Jesus.
O clement, O loving, O sweet Virgin Mary.

V. Pray for us, O holy Mother of God.
R. That we may be made worthy of
the promises of Christ.

43

Oratio quae Dicatur post Rosarium

Deus, cuius Unigenitus per vitam,
mortem, et resurrectionem suam
nobis salutis aeternae praemia
comparavit, concede, quaesumus,
ut haec mysteria sacratissimo
beatae Mariae Virginis Rosario
recolentes, et imitemur quod
continent, et quod promittunt
assequamur. Per eundem
Christum dominum
nostrum.
Amen.

Concluding Prayer

Let us pray.
O God, Whose Only-Begotten Son,
by His life, death and resurrection,
has purchased for us the rewards of
eternal life, grant, we beseech Thee,
that by meditating upon these
mysteries of the most holy Rosary
of the Blessed Virgin Mary, that
we may imitate what they contain,
and obtain what they promise,
through the same Christ our Lord.
Amen.

Sancte Michael Archangele

Sancte Michael Archangele,
defende nos in proelio;
contra nequitiam et insidias diaboli
esto praesidium.
Imperet illi Deus supplices deprecamur:
tuque, Princeps militiae coelestis,
Satanam aliosque spiritus malignos,
qui ad perditionem
animarum pervagantur in mundo,
divina virtute in
infernum detrude.
Amen.

Prayer to Saint Michael the Archangel

Saint Michael the Archangel,
defend us in battle, be our defense
against the wickedness and snares
of the devil; may God rebuke him,
we humbly pray; and do thou,
O Prince of the heavenly host,
by the power of God,
cast into hell Satan
and all evil spirits who
prowl about the world
seeking the ruin of souls.
Amen.

The
Holy Rosary

The Joyful Mysteries

The Annunciation
Blessed Fra Angelico (1387 - 1455)

Mary, the Ark of the New Covenant

O noble Virgin, truly you are great - er than any other greatness. For who is your equal in greatness, O dwelling place of the Word? To whom among all creatures shall I compare you, O Virgin? You are greater than them all. O Covenant, clothed in purity instead of gold! You are the Ark in which is found the golden vessel containing the true manna, that is, the flesh in which divinity resides. Should I compare you to the fertile earth and its fruits? You surpass them, for it is written: "The earth is my footstool" (Isaiah 66:1). But you carry within you the feet, the head, and the entire body of the perfect God.

—Saint Athanasius of Alexandria (296 - 373)
Doctor of the Church
Father of the Church

Primum Mysterium Gaudiosum

 # Annuntiatio

Fructus Mysteriii: Humilitas

 ## Pater Noster

Inimicitias ponam inter te et mulierem, Et semen tuum et semen illius: ipsa conteret caput tuum, et tu insidiaberis calcaneo ejus. Genesis 3:15

Et tu, Bethlehem Ephrata; ex te mihi egredietur qui sit dominator in Israel, et egressus ejus ab initio, a diebus aeternitatis. Michaeas 5:2

 ## Ave Maria

The First Joyful Mystery

The Annunciation

Fruit of the Mystery: Humility

 Our Father

I will put enmities between thee and the woman, and thy seed and her seed: she shall crush thy head, and thou shalt lie in wait for her heel. Genesis 3:15

Hail Mary

And thou, Bethlehem Ephrata: out of thee shall he come forth unto me that is to be the ruler in Israel: and his going forth is from the beginning, from the days of eternity. Micah 5:2

Hail Mary

Suscitavi ab aquilone, et veniet ab ortu solis;
vocabit nomen meum; et adducet magistratus
quasi lutum, et velut plastes conculcans
humum. Isaias 41:25

Propter hoc dabit Dominus ipse vobis signum: Ecce
virgo concipiet, et pariet filium, et vocabitur
nomen ejus Emmanuel. Isaias 7:14

Dominus dixit ad me: Filius meus es tu; ego
hodie genui te. Postula a me, et dabo tibi
gentes haereditatem tuam, et possessionem
tuam terminos terrae. Psalmus 2:7,8

I have raised up one from the north: and he shall come from the rising of the sun. He shall call upon my name: and he shall make princes to be as dirt, and as the potter treading clay. Isaiah 41:25

Therefore the Lord himself shall give you a sign. Behold a virgin shall conceive and bear a son: and his name shall be called Emmanuel. Isaiah 7:14

The Lord hath said to me: Thou art my son; this day have I begotten thee. Ask of me, and I will give thee the Gentiles for thy inheritance, and the utmost parts of the earth for thy possession. Psalm 2:7,8

Missus est angelus Gabrihel a Deo ... ad virginem et nomen virginis Maria. Et ingressus angelus ad eam dixit have gratia plena Dominus tecum benedicta tu in mulieribus. Lucas 1:26-28

Ave Maria

Quae cum audisset, turbata est in sermone ejus, et cogitabat qualis esset ista salutatio. Et ait angelus ei: Ne timeas, Maria: invenisti enim gratiam apud Deum. Lucas 1:29,30

Ave Maria

Ecce concipies in utero, et paries filium, et vocabis nomen ejus Jesum: Hic erit magnus, et Filius Altissimi vocabitur ... et regnabit in domo Jacob in aeternum, et regni ejus non erit finis. Lucas 1:31-33

Ave Maria

The angel Gabriel was sent from God ... to a virgin ... and the virgin's name was Mary. And the angel being come in, said unto her: Hail, full of grace, the Lord is with thee: blessed art thou among women. Luke 1:26-28

Hail Mary

But she was greatly troubled at the saying, and considered in her mind what sort of greeting this might be. And the angel said to her: Do not be afraid, Mary, for you have found favor with God. Luke 1:29,30

Hail Mary

Behold thou shalt conceive in thy womb, and shalt bring forth a son: and thou shalt call his name Jesus. He shall be great, and shall be called Son of the Most High. ... And he shall reign in the house of Jacob forever. And of his kingdom there shall be no end. Luke 1:31-33

Hail Mary

Dixit autem Maria ad angelum: Quomodo fiet
istud, quoniam virum non cognosco? Et respondens
angelus dixit ei: Spiritus Sanctus superveniet
in te, et virtus Altissimi obumbrabit
tibi. Lucas 1:34,35

Dixit autem Maria: Ecce ancilla Domini:
fiat mihi secundum verbum
tuum. ... Lucas 1:38

Gloria Patri, et Filio, et Spiritui Sancto. Sicut
erat in principio, et nunc, et
semper, et in saecula
saeculorum.
Amen.

O mi Jesu, dimitte nobis debita nostra, libera
nos ab igne inferni, conduc in caelum omnes
animas, praesertim illas, quae maxime indigent
misericordia Tua.

And Mary said to the angel: How shall this be done, because I know not man? And the angel answering, said to her: The Holy Ghost shall come upon thee and the power of the most High shall overshadow thee. Luke 1:34,35

Hail Mary

And Mary said: Behold the handmaid of the Lord; be it done to me according to thy word. ... Luke 1:38

Hail Mary

Glory be to the Father, and to the Son, and to the Holy Spirit. As it was in the beginning, is now, and ever shall be. World without end. Amen.

O my Jesus, forgive us our sins, save us from the fires of hell. Lead all souls to heaven, especially those who are most in need of Thy mercy.

The Visitation
Master M. S. (1506)

Perfect Charity

I come now to the soul or life-giving principle of all the virtues. I refer to charity, the virtue alone capable of leading a man to real holiness. In mortifying the flesh, in overcoming sin and in attaining to grace, nothing avails like charity. Would you reach the highest rung of the ladder of perfection? Nothing could possibly be devised to help you more than charity.

In his book on the contemplative life Prosper writes: "Charity is the life of virtue and the death of vice." "As wax melts before the fire" so vices "vanish into nothingness" when they come "face to face" with charity. Charity is a virtue of such power that it can both close the gates of hell and open wide the portals of eternal bliss. Charity provides the hope of salvation and alone renders us lovable in God's sight. It is so great a virtue that among the virtues it is called *the* virtue. ...

Since it is a virtue of supreme importance charity must be insisted on before all else. Let it be well noted, however, that the charity leading to the possession of God is not any charity, but solely *the* charity, the love that loves God above all things and loves God's creatures for God's sake.

The Holy Gospel gives a clear lead on the qualities of this love for God. "Thou shalt love the Lord thy God with thy whole heart, and with thy whole soul, and with thy whole mind." Think well on the love which Your Beloved Jesus demands from you. He desires that you give yourself body and soul, mind and heart entirely to love of Him. He wishes to share your love with no one else. He commands that you be all His. How is this to be done? What are you to do that there can be no doubt that you love the Lord God with your whole heart? How is the love of the whole heart given? For answer, let me quote St. John Chrysostom: "To love God with our whole heart it is requisite that nothing attract your heart more than God attracts it. You must not take more pleasure in the things of earth than in God. Honours and places of position, love of father and mother and relatives must not count in the scale of love before love of God. Be it friend or relative, place or, be it what it may, if anything takes up your heart's love more than God, you do not love God with your whole heart."

—Saint Bonaventure (1221 - 1274)
Doctor of the Church

Secundum Mysterium Gaudiosum

Visitatio

Fructus Mysterii: Dilectio Proximi

 ## Pater Noster

… Aureum habens thuribulum, et arcam testamenti circumtectam ex omni parte auro, in qua urna aurea habens manna, et virga Aaron, quae fronduerat, et tabulae testamenti. Hebraeos 9:4

Ave Maria

Et extimuit David Dominum in die illa, dicens: Quomodo ingredietur ad me arca Domini? 2 Samuelis 6:9

Ave Maria

The Second Joyful Mystery

The Visitation

Fruit of the Mystery: Love of Neighbor

Our Father

... The ark of the testament covered about on every part with gold, in which was a golden pot that had manna and the rod of Aaron that had blossomed and the tables of the testament. Hebrews 9:4

Hail Mary

And David was afraid of the Lord that day, saying: How shall the ark of the Lord come to me? 2 Kings 6:9

Hail Mary

Et habitavit arca Domini in domo Obededom
Gethaei tribus mensibus. ... 2 Samuelis 6:11

Et David saltabat totis viribus ante Dominum. ...
Michol filia Saul ... vidit regem David subsilientem,
atque saltantem coram Domino: et despexit eum in
corde suo. ... Igitur Michol non est natus filius
usque in diem mortis suae. 2 Samuelis 6:14,16,23

Exsurgens autem Maria in diebus illis, abiit in
montana cum festinatione, in civitatem Juda: et
intravit in domum Zachariae, et salutavit
Elisabeth. Lucas 1:39,40

And the ark of the Lord abode in the house of
Obededom the Gethite three months. ... 2 Kings 6:11

And David danced with all his might before the Lord. ...
And ... Michol the daughter of Saul, saw king David
leaping and dancing: and she despised him in her
heart. ... Therefore Michol had no child to
the day of her death. 2 Kings 6:14,16,23

In those days Mary arose and went with haste into the
hill country, to a city of Judah, and she entered
into the house of Zechariah and greeted
Elizabeth. Luke 1:39,40

Et factum est, ut audivit salutationem Mariae
Elisabeth, exsultavit infans in utero
ejus: et repleta est Spiritu Sancto
Elisabeth. Lucas 1:41

Et exclamavit voce magna, et dixit: Benedicta tu inter
mulieres, et benedictus fructus ventris tui. Et unde
hoc mihi, ut veniat mater Domini mei
ad me? Lucas 1:42,43

Ecce enim ut facta est vox salutationis tuae in
auribus meis, exsultavit in gaudio
infans in utero meo. Lucas 1:44

And it came to pass, that when Elizabeth heard the salutation of Mary, the infant leaped in her womb. And Elizabeth was filled with the Holy Ghost. Luke 1:41

And she cried out with a loud voice and said: Blessed art thou among women. And blessed is the fruit of thy womb. And whence is this to me that the mother of my Lord should come to me? Luke 1:42,43

For behold as soon as the voice of thy salution sounded in my ears, the infant in my womb leaped for joy. Luke 1:44

Et ait Maria: Magnificat anima mea Dominum:
Et exsultavit spiritus meus in Deo salutari
meo. Quia respexit humilitatem
ancillae suae. Lucas 1:46-48

Ave Maria

Ecce enim ex hoc beatam me dicent omnes
generationes. Quia fecit mihi magna qui potens
est: et sanctum nomen ejus. ... Mansit autem
Maria cum illa quasi mensibus tribus: et reversa
est in domum suam. Lucas 1:48,49,56

Ave Maria

And Mary said: My soul doth magnify the Lord. And my spirit hath rejoiced in God my Saviour. Because he hath regarded the humility of his handmaid. Luke 1:46-48

Hail Mary

For behold, henceforth all generations will call me blessed. For he who is mighty has done great things for me: and holy is his name. ... And Mary remained with her about three months, and returned to her home. Luke 1:48,49,56

Hail Mary

Gloria Patri, et Filio, et Spiritui Sancto. Sicut
erat in principio, et nunc, et
semper, et in saecula
saeculorum.
Amen.

O mi Jesu, dimitte nobis debita nostra, libera nos
ab igne inferni, conduc in caelum omnes animas,
praesertim illas, quae maxime indigent
misericordia Tua.

Glory be to the Father, and to the Son, and
to the Holy Spirit. As it was in the
beginning, is now, and ever shall
be. World without
end. Amen.

O my Jesus, forgive us our sins, save us from
the fires of hell. Lead all souls to heaven,
especially those who are most in
need of Thy mercy.

Adoration of the Child
Cornelis de Baellieur (1607 - 1671)

The Perpetual Virginity of Mary

It is written (Ezechiel 44:2): 'This gate shall be shut, it shall not be opened, and no man shall pass through it. Because the Lord the God of Israel hath entered in by it … .' What means this closed gate in the house of the Lord, except that Mary is to be ever inviolate? What does it mean that 'no man shall pass through it,' save that Joseph shall not know her? And what is this— 'The Lord alone enters in and goeth out by it,' except that the Holy Ghost shall impregnate her, and that the Lord of Angels shall be born of her? And what means this— 'It shall be shut for evermore,' but that Mary is a Virgin before His birth, a Virgin in His birth, and a Virgin after His birth.

—Saint Augustine (354 - 430)
Father of the Church
Doctor of the Church

Tertium Mysterium Gaudiosum

Nativitas

Fructus Mysterii: Paupertas Spiritualis

Pater Noster

Factum est autem, cum essent
ibi, impleti sunt dies ut pareret. Lucas 2:6

Ave Maria

Et Verbum caro factum est, et habitavit in
nobis … plenum gratiae et
veritatis. Joannes 1:14

Ave Maria

The Third Joyful Mystery

The Nativity

Fruit of the Mystery: Spiritual Poverty

 ## Our Father

And while they were there, the time came for her to be delivered. Luke 2:6

Hail Mary

And the Word was made flesh and dwelt among us ... full of grace and truth. John 1:14

 # Hail Mary

Cum enim quietum silentium contineret omnia, et nox in suo cursu medium iter haberet, omnipotens sermo tuus de caelo, a regalibus sedibus, durus debellator in mediam exterminii terram prosilivit. Sapientia 18:14,15

Ave Maria

Et peperit filium suum primogenitum, et pannis eum involvit, et reclinavit eum in praesepio: quia non erat eis locus in diversorio. Lucas 2:7

Ave Maria

Et pastores erant in regione eadem vigilantes, et custodientes vigilias noctis super gregem suum. Lucas 2:8

Ave Maria

For while all things were in quiet silence and the night
was in the midst of her course, thy almighty word
leapt down from heaven from thy royal throne, as
a fierce conqueror into the midst of the land
of destruction. Wisdom 18:14,15

And she brought forth her firstborn son, and
wrapped him up in swaddling clothes. And laid
him in a manger; because there was no room
for them in the inn. Luke 2:7

And there were in the same country shepherds
watching and keeping the night watches
over their flock. Luke 2:8

Et ecce angelus Domini stetit juxta illos, et claritas Dei circumfulsit illos, et timuerunt timore magno. Lucas 2:9

Ave Maria

Et dixit illis angelus: Nolite timere: ecce enim evangelizo vobis gaudium magnum, quod erit omni populo: Quia natus est vobis hodie Salvator, qui est Christus Dominus, in civitate David. Lucas 2:10,11

Ave Maria

Et subito facta est cum angelo multitudo militiae caelestis laudantium Deum, et dicentium: Gloria in altissimis Deo, et in terra pax hominibus bonae voluntatis. Lucas 2:13,14

Ave Maria

And behold, an angel of the Lord stood by them and the brightness of God shone round about them: and they feared with a great fear. Luke 2:9

And the angel said to them: Fear not; for, behold, I bring you good tidings of great joy that shall be to all the people: For, this day, is born to you a Saviour, who is Christ the Lord, in the city of David. Luke 2:10,11

And suddenly there was with the angel a multitude of the heavenly army, praising God, and saying: Glory to God in the highest: and on earth peace to men of good will.

Luke 2:13,14

Ecce magi ab oriente venerunt Jerusalem. Dicentes: Ubi est qui natus est rex Judaeorum? … Et intrantes domum invenerunt puerum cum Maria matre ejus. Matthaeus 2:1,2,11

Et procidentes adoraverunt eum: et apertis thesauris suis obtulerunt ei munera, aurum, thus, et murram. Matthaeus 2:11

Gloria Patri, et Filio, et Spiritui Sancto. Sicut erat in principio, et nunc, et semper, et in saecula saeculorum. Amen.

O mi Jesu, dimitte nobis debita nostra, libera nos ab igne inferni, conduc in caelum omnes animas, praesertim illas, quae maxime indigent misericordia Tua.

There came wise men from the east to Jerusalem.
Saying, Where is he that is born king of the
Jews?... And entering into the house, they found
the child with Mary his mother. Matthew 2:1,2,11

Hail Mary

And falling down they adored him. And opening
their treasures, they offered him gifts: gold,
frankincense, and myrrh. Matthew 2:11

Hail Mary

Glory be to the Father, and to the Son, and to
the Holy Spirit. As it was in the beginning, is
now, and ever shall be. World
without end. Amen.

O my Jesus, forgive us our sins, save us from
the fires of hell. Lead all souls to heaven,
especially those who are most in
need of Thy mercy.

The Presentation
in the Temple
Lodovico Carracci (1555 - 1619)

Perfect Obedience

Take a corpse and bring it where thou wilt! It makes no resistance, does not change its attitude, does not wish to move. If thou place it on a throne, it looks down and not up; if thou dress it in purple, it appears only paler than before. It is so with the really obedient; he never asks whither he is sent, he never is concerned as to how he came here, and does not seek to be taken away. If he acquires honors, they only increase his humility, and the more he is praised, the more unworthy does he consider himself.

—Saint Francis of Assisi (c. 1181 - 1226)

Quartum Mysterium Gaudiosum

Presentatio

Fructus Mysterii: Oboedientia

Pater Noster

Locutusque est Dominus ad
Moysen, dicens: Sanctifica mihi omne primogenitum
quod aperit vulvam in filiis Israel. ... Exodus 13:1,2

Ave Maria

Loquere filiis Israel, et dices ad eos: Mulier, si
suscepto semine pepererit masculum, immunda
erit septem diebus. ... Leviticus 12:2

Ave Maria

The Fourth Joyful Mystery

The Presentation

Fruit of the Mystery: Obedience

 Our Father

And the Lord spoke to Moses, saying: Sanctify unto me every firstborn that openeth the womb among the children of Israel. ... Exodus 13:1,2

 **Hail Mary**

Speak to the children of Israel, and thou shalt say to them: If a woman having received seed shall bear a man child, she shall be unclean seven days. ... Leviticus 12:2

 **Hail Mary**

Ipsa vero triginta tribus diebus manebit in sanguine purificationis suae. Omne sanctum non tanget, nec ingredietur in sanctuarium, donec impleantur dies purificationis suae. Leviticus 12:4

Et postquam impleti sunt dies purgationis ejus secundum legem Moysi, tulerunt illum in Jerusalem, ut sisterent eum Domino. ... Et ecce homo erat in Jerusalem, cui nomen Simeon, et homo iste justus, et timoratus, exspectans consolationem Israel. Lucas 2:22,25

Et responsum acceperat a Spiritu Sancto, non visurum se mortem, nisi prius videret Christum Domini. Lucas 2:26

But she shall remain three and thirty days in the blood of her purification. She shall touch no holy thing: neither shall she enter into the sanctuary, until the days of her purification be fulfilled. Leviticus 12:4

After the days of her purification, according to the law of Moses, were accomplished, they carried him to Jerusalem, to present him to the Lord. … And behold there was a man in Jerusalem named Simeon: and this man was just and devout, waiting for the consolation of Israel. Luke 2:22,25

And he had received an answer from the Holy Ghost, that he should not see death before he had seen the Christ of the Lord. Luke 2:26

... Et cum inducerent puerum Jesum parentes ejus, ut facerent secundum consuetudinem legis pro eo, et ipse accepit eum in ulnas suas: et benedixit Deum, Et dixit: Nunc dimittis servum tuum Domine, secundum verbum tuum in pace. Lucas 2:27-29

Quia viderunt oculi mei salutare tuum, quod parasti ante faciem omnium populorum: lumen ad revelationem gentium, et gloriam plebis tuae Israel. Lucas 2:30-32

Et benedixit illis Simeon, et dixit ad Mariam matrem ejus: Ecce positus est hic in ruinam, et in resurrectionem multorum in Israel, et in signum cui contradicetur. Lucas 2:34

… And when his parents brought in the child Jesus, to do for him according to the custom of the law, he also took him into his arms, and blessed God and said: Now thou dost dismiss thy servant, O Lord, according to thy word in peace. Luke 2:27-29

Because my eyes have seen thy salvation, which thou hast prepared before the face of all peoples: A light to the revelation of the Gentiles and the glory of thy people Israel. Luke 2:30-32

And Simeon blessed them and said to Mary his mother: Behold this child is set for the fall and for the resurrection of many in Israel and for a sign which shall be contradicted. Luke 2:34

Et tuam ipsius animam pertransibit gladius
ut revelentur ex multis cordibus
cogitationes. Lucas 2:35

Et ut perfecerunt omnia secundum legem
Domini, reversi sunt in Galilaeam in civitatem suam
Nazareth. Puer autem crescebat, et confortabatur
plenus sapientia: et gratia Dei erat
in illo. Lucas 2:39,40

Gloria Patri, et Filio, et Spiritui Sancto. Sicut
erat in principio, et nunc, et
semper, et in saecula
saeculorum.
Amen.

O mi Jesu, dimitte nobis debita nostra, libera
nos ab igne inferni, conduc in caelum omnes
animas, praesertim illas, quae maxime indigent
misericordia Tua.

And thy own soul a sword shall pierce, that, out
of many hearts, thoughts may be
revealed. Luke 2:35

And after they had performed all things according to the
law of the Lord, they returned into Galilee, to their city
of Nazareth. And the child grew and waxed strong,
full of wisdom: and the grace of God was
in him. Luke 2:39,40

Glory be to the Father, and to the Son, and
to the Holy Spirit. As it was in the
beginning, is now, and ever
shall be. World without
end. Amen.

O my Jesus, forgive us our sins, save us from
the fires of hell. Lead all souls to heaven,
especially those who are most in
need of Thy mercy.

Christ in the Temple

Heinrich Hofmann (1824 - 1911)

Seeking Jesus

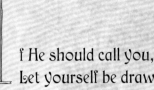

I f He should call you,
    Let yourself be drawn to Him.
He may lead you to a great truth.
Do not dwell on yourself, nor should you —
A creature subject to multiplicity and
    change—seek Him;
rest in tranquility, loftier than action or
    feeling,
And you will find that as you lose yourself
He will give you strength.

Be pleased to remain where it pleases Him
    to place you.
Straining to find Him is of no avail;
Be at peace with yourself. If He embraces
    you,
Return His embrace, but do not feel
    wronged
When He absents Himself. Give no thought
    to yourself;
If you love as you should, you will be filled

with joy,
Because that love in itself
Glows with a light that does not fail.

You know that you can only possess
To the extent that He will give;
What He withholds you cannot acquire;
Nor can you hold onto what you have
Unless He grants you that grace.
Your path from beginning to end
Lies beyond your power;
The choice is not yours but the Lord's.

Hence, if you have found Him know in truth
That it was through no power of yours.
The good that is given you
Comes out of charity; it is a gift,
Not the fruit of your own efforts.
Let all your desire, then,
Be directed toward Him,

The Infinite One, Giver of all good.

—Blessed Jacopone Da Todi
(c. 1230 - 1306)

Quintum Mysterium Gaudiosum

Inventio Pueri Jesu in Templo

Fructus Mysterii: Studium Dei

 ## Pater Noster

Et ibant parentes ejus per omnes annos in Jerusalem, in die solemni Paschae. Et cum factus esset annorum duodecim, ascendentibus illis Jerusalem secundum consuetudinem diei festi. Lucas 2:41,42

Ave Maria

Consummatisque diebus, cum redirent, remansit puer Jesus in Jerusalem, et non cognoverunt parentes ejus. Lucas 2:43

Ave Maria

The Fifth Joyful Mystery

The Finding of the Child Jesus in the Temple

Fruit of the Mystery: Zeal for God

Our Father

Now his parents went to Jerusalem every year at the feast of the Passover. And when he was twelve years old, they went up according to custom. Luke 2:41,42

Hail Mary

And having fulfilled the days, when they returned, the child Jesus remained in Jerusalem. And his parents knew it not. Luke 2:43

Hail Mary

Existimantes autem illum esse in comitatu, venerunt iter diei, et requirebant eum inter cognatos et notos. Et non invenientes, regressi sunt in Jerusalem, requirentes eum. Lucas 2:44,45

... Quaesivi quem diligit anima mea: quaesivi illum, et non inveni. Surgam, et circuibo civitatem: per vicos et plateas quaeram quem diligit anima mea: quaesivi illum, et non inveni. Canticum 3:1,2

... Quaesivi, et non inveni illum; vocavi, et non respondit mihi.
Canticum 5:6

But supposing him to be in the company they went a day's journey, and they sought him among their kinsfolk and acquaintances; and when they did not find him, they returned to Jerusalem, seeking him. Luke 2:44,45

Hail Mary

… I sought him, and found him not. I will rise and will go about the city. In the streets and the broad ways I will seek him whom my soul loveth. I sought him, and I found him not. Song of Songs 3:1,2

Hail Mary

… I sought him and found him not: I called and he did not answer me.
Song of Songs 5:6

Hail Mary

Adjuro vos, filiae Jerusalem, si inveneritis dilectum meum, ut nuntietis ei quia amore langueo. … Quo abiit dilectus tuus, o pulcherrima mulierum? Quo declinavit dilectus tuus? Et quaeremus eum tecum.

Canticum 5:8,17

Et factum est, post triduum invenerunt illum in templo sedentem in medio doctorum, audientem illos, et interrogantem eos. Stupebant autem omnes qui eum audiebant, super prudentia et responsis ejus. Lucas 2:46,47

Et videntes admirati sunt. Fili, quid fecisti nobis sic? Ecce pater tuus et ego dolentes quaerebamus te. Lucas 2:48

I adjure you, O daughters of Jerusalem, if you find my beloved, that you tell him that I languish with love. … Whither is thy beloved gone, O thou most beautiful among women? Whither is thy beloved turned aside, and we will seek him with thee? Song of Songs 5:8,17

And it came to pass that, after three days, they found him in the temple, sitting in the midst of the doctors, hearing them and asking them questions. And all that heard him were astonished at his wisdom and his answers. Luke 2:46,47

And seeing him, they wondered. And his mother said to him: Son, why has thou done so to us? Behold thy father and I have sought thee sorrowing. Luke 2:48

Et ait ad illos: Quid est quod me quaerebatis?
Nesciebatis quia in his quae Patris mei sunt oportet
me esse? Et ipsi non intellexerunt verbum quod
locutus est ad eos. Lucas 2:49,50

Et descendit cum eis, et venit Nazareth: Et erat
subditus illis. Et mater ejus conservabat omnia
verba haec in corde suo. Et Jesus proficiebat
sapientia, et aetate, et gratia apud
Deum et homines. Lucas 2:51,52

Gloria Patri, et Filio, et Spiritui Sancto. Sicut
erat in principio, et nunc, et
semper, et in saecula
saeculorum.
Amen.

O mi Jesu, dimitte nobis debita nostra, libera
nos ab igne inferni, conduc in caelum omnes
animas, praesertim illas, quae maxime indigent
misericordia Tua.

And he said to them: How is it that you sought me? Did you not know that I must be about my father's business? And they understood not the word that he spoke unto them. Luke 2:49,50

Hail Mary

And he went down with them and came to Nazareth, and was obedient to them; and his mother kept all these things in her heart. And Jesus increased in wisdom and in stature, and in favor with God and man. Luke 2:51,52

Hail Mary

Glory be to the Father, and to the Son, and to the Holy Spirit. As it was in the beginning, is now, and ever shall be. World without end. Amen.

O my Jesus, forgive us our sins, save us from the fires of hell. Lead all souls to heaven, especially those who are most in need of Thy mercy.

The Sorrowful
Mysteries

Christ in the Garden of Gethsemane

Sebastiano Conca (1680 - 1746)

Divine Mercy

y mercy is greater than your sins and those of the entire world. ... For you I descended from heaven to earth; for you I allowed myself to be nailed to the cross; for you I let my Sacred Heart be pierced with a lance, thus opening wide the source of mercy for you. Come, then, with trust to draw graces from this fountain. I never reject a contrite heart. Your misery has disappeared in the depths of My mercy. ... You will give me pleasure if you hand over to me all your troubles and griefs. I shall heap upon you the treasures of My grace.

—Private revelation given by Jesus to
Saint Faustina Kowalska (1905 - 1938)

Primum Mysterium Dolorosum

Agonia in Horto

Fructus Mysterii: Dolor Peccatorum

Pater Noster

… Propter scelus populi mei percussi eum. … Et Dominus voluit conterere eum in infirmitate. Isaias 53:8,10

Ave Maria

… In scientia sua justificabit ipse justus servus meus multos, et iniquitates eorum ipse portabit. Isaias 53:11

Ave Maria

The First Sorrowful Mystery

The Agony in the Garden

Fruit of the Mystery: Sorrow for Sin

 Our Father

… For the wickedness of my people have I struck him. … And the Lord was pleased to bruise him in infirmity. Isaiah 53:8,10

 Hail Mary

… By his knowledge shall this my just servant justify many: and he shall bear their iniquities. Isaiah 53:11

 **Hail Mary**

Sicut pullus hirundinis, sic clamabo; meditabor ut columba. Attenuati sunt oculi mei, suspicientes in excelsum. Domine, vim patior, responde pro me. Isaias 38:14

Ave Maria

Et egressus ibat secundum consuetudinem in montem Olivarum. Secuti sunt autem illum et discipuli. Et cum pervenisset ad locum, dixit illis: Orate ne intretis in tentationem. Lucas 22:39,40

Ave Maria

Et progressus pusillum, procidit in faciem suam, orans, et dicens: Pater mi, si possibile est, transeat a me calix iste: verumtamen non sicut ego volo, sed sicut tu. Matthaeus 26:39

Ave Maria

I will cry like a young swallow, I will meditate
like a dove: my eyes are weakened looking
upward. Lord, I suffer violence,
answer thou for me. Isaiah 38:14

Hail Mary

Going out, he went, according to his custom, to
the Mount of Olives. And his disciples also followed
him. And when he was come to the place, he said to
them: Pray, lest ye enter into temptation.
Luke 22:39,40

Hail Mary

And going a little further, he fell upon his face, praying
and saying: My Father, if it be possible, let this
chalice pass from me. Nevertheless, not
as I will, but as thou wilt. Matthew 26:39

Hail Mary

Apparuit autem illi angelus de caelo, confortans eum. Et factus in agonia, prolixius orabat. Et factus est sudor ejus sicut guttae sanguinis decurrentis in terram. Lucas 22:43,44

Et cum surrexisset ab oratione et venisset ad discipulos suos, invenit eos dormientes prae tristitia. Lucas 22:45

Et ait illis: Quid dormitis? Surgite, orate, ne intretis in tentationem.
Lucas 22:46

And there appeared to him an angel from heaven, strengthening him. And being in agony, he prayed the longer. And his sweat became as drops of blood, trickling down upon the ground. Luke 22:43,44

Hail Mary

And when he rose up from prayer, and was come to the disciples, he found them sleeping for sorrow. Luke 22:45

Hail Mary

And he said to them: Why sleep you? Arise: pray: lest you enter into temptation.
Luke 22:46

Hail Mary

… Et qui vocabatur Judas, unus de duodecim, antecedebat eos, et appropinquavit Jesu ut oscularetur eum. Jesus autem dixit illi: Juda osculo Filium hominis tradis? Lucas 22:47,48

Ave Maria

Tunc accesserunt, et manus injecerunt in Jesum, et tenuerunt eum. Tunc discipuli ejus relinquentes eum, omnes fugerunt. Matthaeus 26:50; Marcus 14:50

Ave Maria

Gloria Patri, et Filio, et Spiritui Sancto. Sicut erat in principio, et nunc, et semper, et in saecula saeculorum. Amen.

O mi Jesu, dimitte nobis debita nostra, libera nos ab igne inferni, conduc in caelum omnes animas, praesertim illas, quae maxime indigent misericordia Tua.

... And he that was called Judas, one of the twelve, went before them and drew near to Jesus, for to kiss him. And Jesus said to him: Judas, dost thou betray the Son of man with a kiss? Luke 22:47,48

Hail Mary

Then they came up and laid hands on Jesus and held him. Then his disciples, leaving him, all fled away. Matthew 26:50; Mark 14:50

Hail Mary

Glory be to the Father, and to the Son, and to the Holy Spirit. As it was in the beginning, is now, and ever shall be. World without end. Amen.

O my Jesus, forgive us our sins, save us from the fires of hell. Lead all souls to heaven, especially those who are most in need of Thy mercy.

The Flagellation of Christ
William-Adolphe Bouguereau
(1825 - 1905)

Self-Denial

Unless you completely renounce yourself, my son, perfect freedom cannot be yours. What chains bind those who think only of themselves; the greedy, the inquisitive, the gadabouts, those who look for a soft time, and not for Jesus Christ, those who spend their time planning and fashioning things which have no permanence! Yes, everything that has not come from God will pass completely away. Here is a little bit of sound advice: Give up everything, and you shall find everything; renounce desire, and you shall discover peace. Turn that over in your mind; when you have done what it says, you will understand everything.

—Thomas à Kempis (1379 - 1471)

Secundum Mysterium Dolorosum

Flagellatio ad Columnam

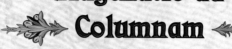

Fructus Mysterii: Munditia

 Pater Noster

Tunc ergo apprehendit Pilatus Jesum, et flagellavit. Joannes 19:1

 Ave Maria

Concidit me vulnere super vulnus: irruit in me quasi gigas. Job 16:15

 Ave Maria

Sicut obstupuerunt super te multi sic inglorius erit inter viros aspectus ejus, et forma ejus inter filios hominum. ... Non est species ei, neque decor. ... Isaias 52:14; 53:2

 Ave Maria

The Second Sorrowful Mystery

The Scourging at the Pillar

Fruit of the Mystery: Purity

 Our Father

Then therefore, Pilate took Jesus and scourged him. John 19:1

 Hail Mary

He hath torn me with wound upon wound: he hath rushed in upon me like a giant. Job 16:15

 Hail Mary

As many have been astonished at thee, so shall his visage be inglorious among men and his form among the sons of men. ... There is no beauty in him, nor comeliness. ... Isaiah: 52:14; 53:2

 Hail Mary

Aestimatus sum cum descendentibus in lacum, factus sum sicut homo sine adjutorio. ... Posuerunt me in lacu inferiori, in tenebrosis, et in umbra mortis. Psalmus 87:5,7

Ave Maria

Longe fecisti notos meos a mei, posuerunt me abominationem sibi.

Psalmus 87:9

Ave Maria

Despectum, et novissimum virorum, virum dolorum, et scientem infirmitatem.

Isaias 53:3

Ave Maria

Et quasi absconditus vultus ejus et despectus, unde nec reputavimus eum. Isaias 53:3

Ave Maria

I am counted among them that go down to the pit: I am become as a man without help. ... They have laid me in the lower pit: in the dark places, and in the shadow of death. Psalm 87:5,7

Hail Mary

Thou hast put away my acquaintance far from me: They have set me an abomination to themselves. Psalm 87:9

Hail Mary

Despised and the most abject of men, a man of sorrows, and acquainted with infirmity.

Isaiah 53:3

Hail Mary

And his look was as it were hidden and despised. Whereupon we esteemed him not. Isaiah 53:3

 Hail Mary

Pelli meae, consumptis carnibus, adhaesit os meum, et derelicta sunt tantummodo labia circa dentes meos. Miseremini mei, miseremini mei, saltem vos, amici mei, quia manus Domini tetigit me. Job 19:20,21

... Et nos putavimus eum quasi leprosum, et percussum a Deo, et humiliatum. Ipse autem vulneratus est propter iniquitates nostras, attritus est propter scelera nostra; disciplina pacis nostrae super eum, et livore ejus sanati sumus. Isaias 53:4,5

... Si posuerit pro peccato animam suam, videbit semen longaevum, et voluntas Domini in manu ejus dirigetur. Isaias 53:10

The flesh being consumed, my bone hath cleaved to my skin, and nothing but lips are left about my teeth. Have pity on me, have pity on me, at least you my friends, because the hand of the Lord hath touched me. Job 19:20,21

 **Hail Mary**

… And we have thought him as it were a leper, and as one struck by God and afflicted. But he was wounded for our iniquities: he was bruised for our sins. The chastisement of our peace was upon him: and by his bruises we are healed. Isaiah 53:4,5

 **Hail Mary**

… If he shall lay down his life for sin, he shall see a long-lived seed: and the will of the Lord shall be prosperous in his hand. Isaiah 53:10

 **Hail Mary**

125

Gloria Patri, et Filio, et Spiritui Sancto.
Sicut erat in principio, et nunc, et
semper, et in saecula
saeculorum.
Amen.

O mi Jesu, dimitte nobis debita nostra, libera
nos ab igne inferni, conduc in caelum
omnes animas, praesertim
illas, quae maxime indigent
misericordia
Tua.

Glory be to the Father, and to the Son, and
to the Holy Spirit. As it was in the
beginning, is now, and ever
shall be. World without
end. Amen.

O my Jesus, forgive us our sins, save
us from the fires of hell. Lead
all souls to heaven, especially
those who are most in
need of Thy
mercy.

The Crowning with Thorns
Maarten van Heemskerk (1498 - 1574)

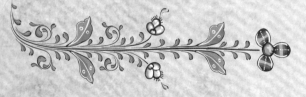

The Virtue of Courage

I call Almighty God to witness, and I beseech all here present to attest for me on the dreadful danger of judgment, that, being about to die in public, I declare that I have refused to comply with the will of His Majesty the King, not from obstinacy, malice, or a rebellious spirit, but solely for fear of offending the supreme Majesty of God. Our holy Mother the Church has decreed and enjoined otherwise than the king and Parliament have decreed. I am therefore bound in conscience, and am ready and willing to suffer every kind of torture, rather than deny a doctrine of the Church. Pray for me, and have mercy on my brethren, of whom I have been the unworthy Prior.

—Saint John Houghton (c. 1486 - 1535)
Carthusian hermit, priest, and martyr

Tertium Mysterium Dolorosum

Coronatio
Spinis

Fructus Mysterii: Fortitudo

Pater Noster

Quoniam quem tu percussisti persecuti sunt, et
super dolorem vulnerum meorum
addiderunt. Psalmus 68:27

Ave Maria

Corpus meum dedi percutientibus, et genas
meas vellentibus; faciem meam non
averti ab increpantibus et
conspuentibus in me. Isaias 50:6

Ave Maria

The Third Sorrowful Mystery

The Crowning With Thorns

Fruit of the Mystery: Courage

Our Father

They have persecuted him whom thou hast smitten: and they have added to the grief of my wounds. Psalm 68:27

Hail Mary

I have given my body to the strikers, and my cheeks to them that plucked them: I have not turned away my face from them that rebuked me and spit upon me. Isaiah 50:6

Hail Mary

Oblatus est quia ipse voluit, et non aperuit os suum; sicut ovis ad occisionem ducetur, et quasi agnus coram tondente se obmutescet .... Isaias 53:7

Tunc milites praesidis suscipientes Jesum in praetorium, congregaverunt ad eum universam cohortem: Et exuentes eum, chlamydem coccineam cicumdederunt ei. Matthaeus 27:27,28

Et plectentes coronam de spinis, posuerunt super caput ejus, et arundinem in dextera ejus. Matthaeus 27:29

He was offered because it was his own will, and
he opened not his mouth. He shall be led as a
sheep to the slaughter and shall be dumb as
a lamb before his shearer .... Isaiah 53:7

Then the soldiers of the governor took Jesus into the
praetorium, and they gathered the whole battalion
before him. And they stripped him and put
a scarlet robe upon him.
Matthew 27:27,28

And platting a crown of thorns, they put it
upon his head, and a reed in his
right hand. Matthew 27:29

Et genu flexo ante eum, illudebant ei, dicentes: Ave rex Judaeorum. Et exspuentes in eum, acceperunt arundinem, et percutiebant caput ejus. Matthaeus 27:29,30

 **Ave Maria**

Exivit ergo Jesus portans coronam spineam, et purpureum vestimentum. Et [Pilatus] dicit eis: Ecce homo. Joannes 19:5

 **Ave Maria**

Cum ergo vidissent eum pontifices et ministri, clamabant, dicentes: Crucifige, crucifige eum … . Joannes 19:6

 **Ave Maria**

And bowing the knee before him, they mocked him, saying: Hail, King of the Jews. And spitting upon him, they took the reed and struck his head. Matthew 27:29,30

So Jesus came out, wearing the crown of thorns and the purple robe. Pilate said to them: Here is the man! John 19:5

When the chief priests, therefore, and the servants had seen him, they cried out, saying: Crucify him, Crucify him … . John 19:6

… Dicit eis Pilatus: Regem vestrum crucifigam? Responderunt pontifices: Non habemus regem, nisi Caesarem. Joannes 19:15

Ave Maria

Tunc ergo tradidit eis illum ut crucifigeretur. Susceperunt autem Jesum, et eduxerunt. Joannes 19:16

Ave Maria

Gloria Patri, et Filio, et Spiritui Sancto. Sicut erat in principio, et nunc, et semper, et in saecula saeculorum. Amen

O mi Jesu, dimitte nobis debita nostra, libera nos ab igne inferni, conduc in caelum omnes animas, praesertim illas, quae maxime indigent misericordia Tua.

... Pilate saith to them: Shall I crucify your king? The chief priests answered: We have no king but Caesar. John 19:15

Hail Mary

Then therefore he delivered him to them to be crucified. And they took Jesus and led him forth. John 19:16

Hail Mary

Glory be to the Father, and to the Son, and to the Holy Spirit. As it was in the beginning, is now, and ever shall be. World without end. Amen.

O my Jesus, forgive us our sins, save us from the fires of hell. Lead all souls to heaven, especially those who are most in need of Thy mercy.

Christ Carrying
the Cross
Lorenzo Lotto (1480 - 1556)

The Fewness of Those Who Love the Cross of Jesus

Jesus today has many who love His heavenly kingdom, but few who carry His cross; many who yearn for comfort, few who long for distress. Plenty of people He finds to share His banquet, few to share His fast. Everyone desires to take part in His rejoicing, but few are willing to suffer anything for His sake. There are many that follow Jesus as far as the breaking of bread, few as far as drinking the cup of suffering; many that revere His miracles, few that follow Him in the indignity of His cross; many that love Jesus as long as nothing runs counter to them; many that praise and bless Him, as long as they receive some comfort from Him; but should Jesus hide from them and leave them for a while, they fall to complaining or become depressed.

—Thomas à Kempis (1379 - 1471)

Quartum Mysterium Dolorosum

Bajulatio Crucis

Fructus Mysterii: Patientia

Pater Noster

O vos omnes qui transitis per viam, attendite, et videte si est dolor sicut dolor meus … !

Lamentationes 1:12

Ave Maria

Miser factus sum et curvatus sum usque in finem; tota die contristatus ingrediebar. Psalmus 37:7

Ave Maria

The Fourth Sorrowful Mystery

The Carrying of the Cross

Fruit of the Mystery: Patience

 Our Father

O all ye that pass by the way, attend, and see
if there be any sorrow like to my sorrow ... .
Lamentations 1:12

 Hail Mary

I am become miserable, and am bowed down
even to the end: I walked sorrowful
all the day long. Psalm 37:7

 **Hail Mary**

Omnes nos quasi oves erravimus, unusquisque
in viam suam declinavit; et posuit Dominus
in eo iniquitatem omnium
nostrum. Isaias 53:6

… Infirmata est virtus mea: dedit me
Dominus in manu de qua non potero
surgere. Lamentationes 1:14

Et postquam illuserunt ei, exuerunt illum purpura, et
induerunt eum vestimentis suis: et educunt illum
ut crucifigerent eum. Et bajulans sibi crucem
exivit in eum, qui dicitur Calvariae
locum … . Marcus 15:20; Joannes 19:17

All we like sheep have gone astray, every one
hath turned aside into his own way: and the
Lord hath laid on him the iniquity
of us all. Isaiah 53:6

Hail Mary

… My strength is weakened: the Lord hath delivered
me into a hand out of which I am not able
to rise. Lamentations 1:14

Hail Mary

After they had mocked him, they took off the purple
from him and put his own garments on him: and
they led him out to crucify him. And bearing his
own cross, he went forth to that place which
is called Calvary … . Mark 15:20; John 19:17

Hail Mary

Et cum ducerent eum, apprehenderunt
Simonem quendam Cyrenensem venientem
de villa: et imposuerunt illi crucem portare
post Jesum. Lucas 23:26

Ave Maria

Sequebatur autem illum multa turba populi et mulierum,
quae plangebant et lamentabantur eum. Conversus
autem ad illas Jesus dixit: Filiae Jerusalem, nolite flere
super me, sed super vos ipsas flete et super
filios vestros. Lucas 23:27,28

Ave Maria

Quoniam ecce venient dies in quibus dicent:
Beatae steriles, et ventres qui non
genuerunt … . Quia si in viridi ligno haec
faciunt, in arido quid fiet? Lucas 23:29,31

Ave Maria

And as they led him away, they laid hold of one Simon of Cyrene, coming from the country; and they laid the cross on him to carry after Jesus. Luke 23:26

And there followed him a great multitude of people and of women, who bewailed and lamented him. But Jesus turning to them said: Daughters of Jerusalem, weep not over me; but weep for yourselves and your children. Luke 23:27,28

For behold, the days shall come, wherein they will say: Blessed are the barren and the wombs that have not borne .... For if in the green wood they do these things, what shall be done in the dry? Luke 23:29,31

Dicebat autem ad omnes: Si quis vult post me venire, abneget semetipsum, et tollat crucem suam quotidie, et sequatur me. Lucas 9:23

Et qui non bajulat crucem suam et venit post me, non potest meus esse discipulus. Jugum enim meum suave est, et onus meum leve.
Lucas 14:27; Matthaeus 11:30

Gloria Patri, et Filio, et Spiritui Sancto. Sicut erat in principio, et nunc, et semper, et in saecula saeculorum. Amen.

O mi Jesu, dimitte nobis debita nostra, libera nos ab igne inferni, conduc in caelum omnes animas, praesertim illas, quae maxime indigent misericordia Tua.

And he said to all: If any man will come after me, let him deny himself and take up his cross daily and follow me. Luke 9:23

And whosoever doth not carry his cross and come after me cannot be my disciple. For my yoke is sweet and my burden light.
Luke 14:27; Matthew 11:30

Glory be to the Father, and to the Son, and to the Holy Spirit. As it was in the beginning, is now, and ever shall be. World without end. Amen.

O my Jesus, forgive us our sins, save us from the fires of hell. Lead all souls to heaven, especially those who are most in need of Thy mercy.

The Elevation of the Cross

Peter Paul Rubens (1577 - 1640)

The Cross Contains
All the Love of God

According to an ancient Roman tradition, while fleeing the city during the persecutions of Nero, Saint Peter saw Jesus was travelling in the opposite direction, that is, toward the city, and asked Him in amazement: "Lord, where are you going?" Jesus' response was: "I am going to Rome to be crucified again." At that moment, Peter understood that he had to follow the Lord with courage, to the very end. But he also realized that he would never be alone on the journey; Jesus, who had loved him even unto death, would always be with him. Jesus, with His Cross, walks with us and takes upon Himself our fears, our problems, and our sufferings, even those which are deepest and most painful. With the Cross, Jesus unites Himself to the silence of the victims of violence, those who can no longer cry out, especially the innocent and the defenseless. ...

The Cross of Christ bears the suffering and the sin of mankind, including our own. Jesus accepts all this with open arms, bearing on His shoulders our crosses and saying to us: "Have courage! You do not carry your cross alone! I carry it with you. I have overcome death and I have come to give you hope, to give you life." What has the Cross left in each one of us? You see, it gives us a treasure that no one else can give: the certainty of the faithful love which God has for us. A love so great that it enters into our sin and forgives it, enters into our suffering and gives us the strength to bear it. It is a love which enters into death to conquer it and to save us. The Cross of Christ contains all the love of God; there we find His immeasurable mercy. This is a love in which we can place all our trust, in which we can believe.

... Let us entrust ourselves to Jesus, let us give ourselves over to Him, because He never disappoints anyone! Only in Christ crucified and risen can we find salvation and redemption. With Him,

evil, suffering, and death do not have the last word, because He gives us hope and life: He has transformed the Cross from being an instrument of hate, defeat, and death, to being a sign of love, victory, triumph and life. ... There is no cross, big or small, in our life which the Lord does not share with us.

But the Cross of Christ invites us also to allow ourselves to be smitten by His love, teaching us always to look upon others with mercy and tenderness, especially those who suffer. ... The Cross invites us to step outside ourselves to meet them and to extend a hand to them. How many times have we seen them in the Way of the Cross, how many times have they accompanied Jesus on the way to Calvary: Pilate, Simon of Cyrene, Mary, the women ... . Today I ask you: which of them do you want to be? Do you want to be like Pilate, who did not have the courage to go against the tide to save Jesus' life, and instead washed his hands? Tell me: are you one of those who wash their hands, who feign ignorance and look the

other way? Or are you like Simon of Cyrene, who helped Jesus to carry that heavy wood, or like Mary and the other women, who were not afraid to accompany Jesus all the way to the end, with love and tenderness? And you, who do you want to be? Like Pilate? Like Simon? Like Mary? Jesus is looking at you now and is asking you: do you want to help me carry the Cross? Brothers and sisters, ... how will you respond to Him?

Dear friends, let us bring to Christ's Cross our joys, our sufferings and our failures. There we will find a Heart that is open to us and understands us, forgives us, loves us and calls us to bear this love in our lives, to love each person, each brother and sister, with the same love.

—Pope Francis (1936 -)
Apostolic Reign (2013 -)

152

Quintum Mysterium Dolorosum

Crucifixio

Fructus Mysterii: Perseverantia

Pater Noster

… Tentavit Deus Abraham, et dixit ad eum: Abraham, Abraham. At ille respondit: Adsum. Ait illi:
Tolle filium tuum unigenitum, quem diligis, Isaac, et
vade in terram visionis, atque ibi offeres eum in
holocaustum super unum montium quem
monstravero tibi. Genesis 22:1,2

Ave Maria

Tulit quoque ligna holocausti, et imposuit super
Isaac filium suum: ipse vero portabat
in manibus ignem et gladium. …
Genesis 22:6

Ave Maria

The Fifth Sorrowful Mystery

The Crucifixion

Fruit of the Mystery: Perseverance

 ## Our Father

… God tempted Abraham, and said to him: Abraham, Abraham. And he answered: Here I am. He said to him: Take thy only begotten son Isaac, whom thou lovest, and go into the land of vision: and there thou shalt offer him for an holocaust upon one of the mountains which I will shew thee. Genesis 22:1,2

 ## Hail Mary

And he took the wood for the holocaust, and laid it upon Isaac his son: and he himself carried in his hands fire and a sword. …
Genesis 22:6

 ## Hail Mary

Dixit Isaac patri suo: Pater mi. ... Ubi est victimaholocausti? Dixit autem Abraham: Deus providebit sibi victimam holocausti, fili mi.
Genesis 22:7,8

Et erit in die illa, dicit Dominus Deus: occidet sol in meridie, et tenebrescere faciam terram in die luminis. Amos 8:9

Et postquam venerunt in locum qui vocatur Calvariae, ibi crucifixerunt eum: et latrones, unum a dextris, et alterum a sinistris. Jesus autem dicebat: Pater, dimitte illis: non enim sciunt quid faciunt. ... Lucas 23:33,34

Isaac said to his father: My father. ... Where is the victim for the holocaust? And Abraham said: God will provide himself a victim for an holocaust, my son.

Genesis 22:7,8

Hail Mary

And it shall come to pass in that day, saith the Lord God, that the sun shall go down at midday, and I will make the earth dark in the day of light. Amos 8:9

Hail Mary

When they were come to the place which is called Calvary, they crucified him there: and the robbers, one on the right hand, and the other on the left. And Jesus said: Father, forgive them, for they know not what they do. ... Luke 23:33,34

Hail Mary

Unus autem de his qui pendebant latronibus blasphemabat eum … Respondens autem alter icrepabat illum. Et dicebat ad Jesum: Domine, memento mei cum veneris in regnum tuum. Et dixit illi Jesus: Amen dico tibi: hodie mecum eris in paradiso. Lucas 23:39,40,42,43

Ave Maria

Cum vidisset ergo Jesus matrem, et discipulum stantem, quem diligebat, dicit matri suae: Mulier, ecce filius tuus. Deinde dicit discipulo: Ecce mater tua. Et ex illa hora accepit eam discipulus in sua. Joannes 19:26,27

Ave Maria

A sexta autem hora tenebrae factae sunt super universam terram usque ad horam nonam. Et circa horam nonam clamavit Jesus voce magna, dicens: Eli, Eli, lamma sabacthani? Hoc est … Deus meus, Deus meus, ut quid dereliquisti me? Matthaeus 27:45,46

Ave Maria

And one of those robbers who were hanged, blasphemed him ... But the other answering, rebuked him. ... And he said to Jesus ... Lord, remember me when thou shalt come into thy kingdom. And Jesus said to him: Amen I say to thee: This day thou shalt be with me in paradise. Luke 23:39,40,42,43

Hail Mary

When Jesus therefore had seen his mother and the disciple standing whom he loved, he saith to his mother: Woman, behold thy son. After that, he saith to the disciple: Behold thy mother. And from that hour, the disciple took her to his own. John 19:26,27

Hail Mary

Now from the sixth hour, there was darkness over the whole earth, until the ninth hour. And about the ninth hour Jesus cried with a loud voice ... My God, My God, why hast thou forsaken me? Matthew 27:45,46

Hail Mary

159

Postea sciens Jesus quia omnia consummata sunt, ut consummaretur Scriptura, dixit: Sitio. Illi autem spongiam plenam aceto, hyssopo circumponentes, obtulerunt ori ejus. Cum ergo accepisset Jesus acetum, dixit: Consummatum est. ...

Joannes 19:28-30

 ## Ave Maria

Et clamans voce magna Jesus ait: Pater, in manus tuas commendo spiritum meum. Et haec dicens, exspiravit. Lucas 23:46

 ## Ave Maria

Gloria Patri, et Filio, et Spiritui Sancto. Sicut erat in principio, et nunc, et semper, et in saecula saeculorum.
Amen.

O mi Jesu, dimitte nobis debita nostra, libera nos ab igne inferni, conduc in caelum omnes animas, praesertim illas, quae maxime indigent misericordia Tua.

Afterwards, Jesus knowing that all things were now accomplished, that the scripture might be fulfilled, said: I thirst. And they, putting a sponge full of vinegar and hyssop, put it to his mouth. Jesus therefore, when he had taken the vinegar, said: It is consummated. …
John 19:28-30

Hail Mary

And Jesus crying out with a loud voice said: Father, into thy hands I commend my spirit. And saying this, he gave up the ghost. Luke 23:46

Hail Mary

Glory be to the Father, and to the Son, and to the Holy Spirit. As it was in the beginning, is now, and ever shall be. World without end. Amen.

O my Jesus, forgive us our sins, save us from the fires of hell. Lead all souls to heaven, especially those who are most in need of Thy mercy.

The Glorious Mysteries

Noli Me Tangere
Correggio (1489 - 1534)

"Whose Sins You Shall Forgive..."

arth's inhabitants, having their life in this world, have been entrusted with the stewardship of heavenly things, and have received an authority which God has not given to angels or archangels. Not to them was it said, "What things soever ye shall bind on earth shall be bound also in heaven; and what things soever ye shall loose, shall be loosed" (Matt. 18:18). Those who are lords on earth have indeed the power to bind, but only men's bodies. But this binding touches the very soul and reaches through heaven. What priests do on earth, God ratifies above. The Master confirms the decisions of His slaves. Indeed He has given them nothing less than the whole authority

of heaven. For He says, "Whosoever sins ye retain, they are retained" (John 20:23). What authority could be greater than that? But I see that the Son has placed it all in their hands. For they have been raised to this prerogative, as though they were already translated to heaven and had transcended human nature and were freed from our passions.

—Saint John Chrysostom (c. 347 - 407)
Doctor of the Church
Father of the Church

Primum Mysterium Gloriosum

Resurrectio

Fructus Mysterii: Fides

Pater Noster

Auctorem vero vitae interfecistis, quem
Deus suscitavit a mortuis .... Actus 3:15

Ave Maria

Scio enim quod redemptor meus vivat, et in
novissimo die de terra surrecturus sim: Et
rursum circumdabor pelle mea, et in carne
mea videbo Deum meum. Job 19:25,26

Ave Maria

The First Glorious Mystery

The Resurrection

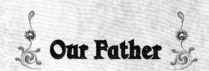

Fruit of the Mystery: Faith

Our Father

The author of life you killed, whom God hath raised from the dead . . . . Acts 3:15

Hail Mary

For I know that my Redeemer liveth, and in the last day I shall rise out of the earth. And I shall be clothed again with my skin: and in my flesh I shall see my God. Job 19:25,26

Hail Mary

... Haec dicit Dominus Deus: Ecce ego aperiam tumu-
los vestros, et educam vos de sepulchris vestris, populus meus, et inducam vos in terram Israel. Et scietis
quia ego Dominus .... Ezechiel 37:12,13

Vivificabit nos post duos dies; in die
tertia suscitabit nos, et vivemus in
conspectu ejus .... Osee 6:3

Una autem sabbati valde diluculo venerunt ad
monumentum, portantes quae paraverant
aromata. Et invenerunt lapidem revolutum
a monumento. Et ingressae non invenerunt
corpus Domini Jesu. Lucas 24:1-3

... Thus saith the Lord God: Behold I will open your graves and will bring you out of your sepulchres, O my people, and will bring you into the land of Israel. And you shall know that I am the Lord ... . Ezekiel 37:12,13

He will revive us after two days: On the third day he will raise us up and we shall live in his sight ... . Hosea 6:3

On the first day of the week, very early in the morning, they came to the sepulchre, bringing the spices which they had prepared. And they found the stone rolled back from the sepulchre. And going in, they found not the body of the Lord Jesus. Luke 24:1-3

Dum mente consternatae essent de isto, ecce duo viri steterunt secus illas in veste fulgenti. Cum timerent autem, et declinarent vultum in terram, dixerunt ad illas: Quid quaeritis viventem cum mortuis? Non est hic, sed surrexit … . Lucas 24:4-6

Cum ergo sero esset die illo, una sabbatorum, et fores essent clausae, ubi erant discipuli congregati propter metum Judaeorum: venit Jesus, et stetit in medio, et dixit eis: Pax vobis. Et cum hoc dixisset, ostendit eis manus et latus … . Joannes 20:19,20

Haec cum dixisset, insufflavit, et dixit eis: Accipite Spiritum Sanctum: quorum remiseritis peccata, remittuntur eis: et quorum retinueritis, retenta sunt. Joannes 20:22,23

As they were astonished in their mind at this, behold, two men stood by them, in shining apparel. And as they were afraid, and bowed down their countenance towards the ground, they said unto them: Why seek you the living with the dead? He is not here, but is risen … . Luke 24:4-6

 **Hail Mary**

Now when it was late that same day, and the doors were shut, where the disciples were gathered together, for fear of the Jews, Jesus came and stood in the midst, and said to them: Peace be to you. And when he had said this, he shewed them his hands and his side … . John 20:19,20

 **Hail Mary**

When he had said this, he breathed on them and said to them: Receive ye the Holy Ghost. Whose sins you shall forgive, they are forgiven them: and whose sins you shall retain, they are retained.

John 20:22,23

 **Hail Mary**

Thomas autem unus ex duodecim, qui dicitur Didymus, non erat cum eis quando venit Jesus. Dixerunt ergo ei alii discipuli: Vidimus Dominum. Ille autem dixit eis: Nisi videro in manibus ejus fixuram clavorum, et mittam digitum meum in locum clavorum, et mittam manum meam in latus ejus, non credam. Joannes 20:24,25

Et post dies octo, iterum erant discipuli ejus intus, et Thomas cum eis. Venit Jesus januis clausis, et stetit in medio, et dixit: Pax vobis. Deinde dicit Thomae: Infer digitum tuum huc, et vide manus meas et affer manum tuam, et mitte in latus meum: et noli esse incredulus, sed fidelis. Respondit Thomas, et dixit ei: Dominus meus et Deus meus.
Joannes 20:26-28

Now Thomas, one of the twelve, was not with them when Jesus came. The other disciples therefore said to him: We have seen the Lord. But he said to them: Except I shall see in his hands the print of the nails and put my finger into the place of the nails and put my hand into his side, I will not believe. John 20:24,25

Hail Mary

And after eight days, again his disciples were within, and Thomas with them. Jesus cometh, the doors being shut, and stood in the midst and said: Peace be to you. Then he said to Thomas: Put in thy finger hither and see my hands. And bring hither thy hand, and put it into my side. And be not faithless, but believing. Thomas answered and said to him: My Lord, and my God.

John 20:26-28

Hail Mary

Gloria Patri, et Filio, et Spiritui Sancto. Sicut
erat in principio, et nunc, et
semper, et in saecula
saeculorum.
Amen.

O mi Jesu, dimitte nobis debita nostra, libera
nos ab igne inferni, conduc in caelum
omnes animas, praesertim
illas, quae maxime indigent
misericordia Tua.

Glory be to the Father, and to the Son,
and to the Holy Spirit. As it was in the
beginning, is now, and ever shall
be. World without
end. Amen.

O my Jesus, forgive us our sins, save us
from the fires of hell. Lead all souls
to heaven, especially those who
are most in need of
Thy mercy.

The Ascension of Christ
Benjamin West (1738 - 1820)

The Virtue of Hope

I f you decide that you are disgusted with yourself, may I say that you can come to God even by a succession of disgusts? What does your disgust mean except that everything earthly has failed you? That is one of the ways God makes you feel hunger for the Divine. Do you not crave food most when you are hungry? Do you not want water most when you are thirsty? Your own disgust, if you knew it, is the distant call of Divine Mercy. If then the poverty of your merits makes you shrink from the Divine Presence, then let your needs draw you to it. And that, incidently, is why we Catholics find comfort and solace in the Sacrament of Penance. When we are disgusted with our sins we can go

179

into a little booth called a confessional box, unload our misery, have our sins washed away, and start life all over again. I know a thousand psychoanalysts who will explain sins away, but that is not what we want. We want them forgiven.

—Venerable Fulton J. Sheen
(1895 - 1979)

Secundum Mysterium Gloriosum

Ascensio

Fructus Mysterii: Spes

Pater Noster

Attollite portas, principes, vestras, et
elevamini, portae aeternales, et introibit
rex gloriae. Psalmus 23:7

 **Ave Maria**

Ascendisti in altum, cepisti captivitatem,
accepisti dona in hominibus.
Psalmus 67:19

 **Ave Maria**

Dixit Dominus Domino meo: Sede a dextris
meis, donec ponam inimicos tuos scabellum
pedum tuorum. Psalmus 109:1

 **Ave Maria**

The Second Glorious Mystery

 ## The Ascension

Fruit of the Mystery: Hope

 ## Our Father

Lift up your gates, O ye princes, and be ye lifted up, O eternal gates: and the King of Glory shall enter in. Psalm 23:7

 ## Hail Mary

Thou hast ascended on high; thou hast led captivity captive; thou hast received gifts in men. Psalm 67:19

 ## Hail Mary

The Lord said to my Lord: Sit thou at my right hand: Until I make thy enemies thy footstool. Psalm 109:1

 ## Hail Mary

Sedes tua, Deus, in saeculum saeculi; virga
directionis virga regni tui.

Psalmus 44:7

 **Ave Maria**

Undecim autem discipuli abierunt in Galilaeam in
montem ubi constituerat illis Jesus. Et videntes eum
adoraverunt: quidam autem dubitaverunt. Et accedens
Jesus locutus est eis, dicens: Data est mihi
omnis potestas in caelo et in terra.

Matthaeus 28:16-18

 **Ave Maria**

Euntes ergo docete omnes gentes: baptizantes eos in
nomine Patris, et Filii, et Spiritus Sancti: docentes eos
servare omnia quaecumque mandavi vobis: et ecce
ego vobiscum sum omnibus diebus, usque
ad consummationem saeculi.

Matthaeus 28:19,20

 **Ave Maria**

Thy throne, O God, is for ever and ever: the sceptre of thy kingdom is a sceptre of uprightness.

Psalm 44:7

Hail Mary

Now the eleven disciples went to Galilee, to the mountain to which Jesus had directed them. And when they saw him they worshiped him; but some doubted. And Jesus came and said to them: All authority in heaven and on earth has been given to me.

Matthew 28:16-18

Hail Mary

Going therefore, teach ye all nations: baptizing them in the name of the Father and of the Son and of the Holy Ghost, teaching them to observe all things whatsoever I have commanded you. And behold I am with you all days, even to the consummation of the world.

Matthew 28:19,20

Hail Mary

Qui crediderit, et baptizatus fuerit, salvus
erit: qui vero non crediderit,
condemnabitur. Marcus 16:16

 **Ave Maria**

Et Dominus quidem Jesus postquam locutus
est eis, assumptus est in caelum, et
sedet a dextris Dei. Marcus 16:19

 **Ave Maria**

Cumque intuerentur in caelum euntem illum, ecce
duo viri astiterunt juxta illos in vestibus albis, qui
et dixerunt: Viri Galilaei, quid statis aspicientes in
caelum? Hic Jesus, qui assumptus est a vobis in
caelum, sic veniet quemadmodum vidistis
eum euntem in caelum. Actus 1:10,11

 **Ave Maria**

He that believeth and is baptized shall be
saved: but he that believeth not shall
be condemned. Mark 16:16

The Lord Jesus, after he had spoken to them, was
taken up into heaven, and sitteth on
the right hand of God. Mark 16:19

And while they were gazing into heaven as he went,
behold, two men stood by them in white robes, and
said: Men of Galilee, why do you stand looking into
heaven? This Jesus, who was taken up from you
into heaven, will come in the same way as you
saw him go into heaven. Acts 1:10,11

... Videbitis Filium hominis sedentem a dextris virtutis Dei, et venientem cum nubibus caeli. Marcus 14:62

Ave Maria

Gloria Patri, et Filio, et Spiritui Sancto. Sicut erat in principio, et nunc, et semper, et in saecula saeculorum. Amen.

O mi Jesu, dimitte nobis debita nostra, libera nos ab igne inferni, conduc in caelum omnes animas, praesertim illas, quae maxime indigent misericordia Tua.

… And you shall see the Son of man sitting on the right hand of the power of God and coming with the clouds of heaven. Mark 14:62

Hail Mary

Glory be to the Father, and to the Son, and to the Holy Spirit. As it was in the beginning, is now, and ever shall be. World without end. Amen.

O my Jesus, forgive us our sins, save us from the fires of hell. Lead all souls to heaven, especially those who are most in need of Thy mercy.

The Pentecost
Waldburg-Wolfegg collection at Wolfegg Castle
Master of the Salem Heilingenaltar
end of the 15th century

The Two Necessary Sanctifiers

The Holy Spirit conveyed the divine fruitfulness of the Father to Mary and this virginal soil brought forth in an ineffable manner our most loving Savior, the Divine Seed, as the prophets called Him. This is what we are taught regarding Jesus, with the conciseness and the precision of an article of Faith: "who was conceived by the Holy Spirit ... of the Virgin Mary." That is the way Jesus is always conceived. That is the way He is reproduced in souls. He is always the fruit of heaven and earth. Two artisans must concur in the work that is at once God's masterpiece and humanity's supreme product: the Holy Spirit and the most holy Virgin Mary. Two sanctifiers are necessary to souls, the Holy Spirit and the Virgin Mary, for they are the only ones who can reproduce Christ.

—Servant of God Luis M. Martinez (1881 - 1956)

191

Tertium Mysterium Gloriosum

Descensus Spiritus Sancti

Fructus Mysterii: Dilectio Dei

Pater Noster

Dabo vobis cor novum, et spiritum novum
ponam in medio vestri: et auferam cor
lapideum de carne vestra, et dabo
vobis cor carneum. Ezechiel 36:26

Ave Maria

Et assumam vos mihi in populum, et ero
vester Deus: et scietis quod ego sum
Dominus Deus … . Exodus 6:7

Ave Maria

The Third Glorious Mystery

The Descent of the Holy Spirit

Fruit of the Mystery: Love of God

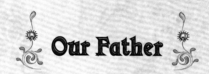

Our Father

I will give you a new heart and put a new spirit
within you: and I will take away the stony
heart out of your flesh and will give
you a heart of flesh. Ezekiel 36:26

Hail Mary

And I will take you to myself for my people.
I will be your God: and you shall know
that I am the Lord your God .... Exodus 6:7

Hail Mary

Et ego rogabo Patrem, et alium Paraclitum dabit vobis, ut maneat vobiscum in aeternum, Spiritum veritatis, quem mundus non potest accipere, quia non videt eum, nec scit eum: vos autem cognoscetis eum, quia apud vos manebit, et in vobis erit. Joannes 14:16,17

 **Ave Maria**

Accipietis virtutem supervenientis Spiritus Sancti in vos, et eritis mihi testes in Jerusalem, et in omni Judaea, et Samaria, et usque ad ultimum terrae. Actus 1:8

 **Ave Maria**

Et cum complerentur dies Pentecostes, erant omnes pariter in eodem loco: et factus est repente de caelo sonus, tamquam advenientis spiritus vehementis, et replevit totam domum ubi erant sedentes. Actus 2:1,2

 **Ave Maria**

And I will ask the Father: and he shall give you another Paraclete, that he may abide with you forever: the spirit of truth, whom the world cannot receive, because it seeth him not, nor knoweth him. But you shall know him; because he shall abide with you and shall be in you. John 14:16,17

You shall receive the power of the Holy Ghost coming upon you, and you shall be witnesses unto me in Jerusalem, and in all Judea and Samaria, and even to the uttermost part of the earth. Acts 1:8

And when the days for the Pentecost were accomplished, they were all in one place. And suddenly there came a sound from heaven, as of a mighty wind coming: and it filled the house where they were sitting. Acts 2:1,2

Et apparuerunt illis dispertitae linguae tamquam ignis, seditque supra singulos eorum: Et repleti sunt omnes Spiritu Sancto, et coeperunt loqui variis linguis, prout Spiritus Sanctus dabat eloqui illis. Actus 2:3,4

Ave Maria

Erant autem in Jerusalem habitantes Judaei, viri religiosi ex omni natione, quae sub caelo est. Facta autem hac voce, convenit multitudo, et mente confusa est, quoniam audiebat unusquisque lingua sua illos loquentes. Actus 2:5,6

Ave Maria

And there appeared to them parted tongues, as it were of fire: and it sat upon every one of them. And they were all filled with the Holy Ghost: and they began to speak with divers tongues, according as the Holy Ghost gave them to speak. Acts 2:3,4

Now there were dwelling in Jerusalem Jews, devout men from every nation under heaven. And at this sound the multitude came together, and they were bewildered, because each one heard them speaking in his own language. Acts 2:5,6

Stupebant autem omnes, et mirabantur ad invicem,
dicentes: Quidnam vult hoc esse?… Stans autem
Petrus cum undecim, levavit vocem suam, et locutus
est eis. … Sed hoc est quod dictum est per
prophetam Joel. … Et quidem super servos meos,
et super ancillas meas in diebus illis effundam
de Spiritu meo … . Actus 2:12,14,16,18

Cum autem audissent Apostoli, qui erant Jerusalem,
quod recepisset Samaria verbum Dei, miserunt ad
eos Petrum et Joannem. Qui cum venissent,
oraverunt pro ipsis ut acciperent
Spiritum Sanctum: nondum enim in quemquam
illorum venerat, sed baptizati tantum erant
in nomine Domini Jesu. Actus 8:14-16

And they were all astonished and wondered, saying one to another: What meaneth this?… But Peter, standing up with the eleven, lifted up his voice and spoke to them. … But this is that which was spoken of by the prophet Joel. … Upon my servants, indeed, and upon my handmaids will I pour out in those days of my spirit … . Acts 2:12,14,16,18

Now, when the apostles, who were in Jerusalem, had heard that Samaria had received the word of God, they sent unto them Peter and John. Who, when they were come, prayed for them that they might receive the Holy Ghost. For he was not yet come upon any of them: but they were only baptized in the name of the Lord Jesus. Acts 8:14-16

Tunc imponebant manus super illos, et
accipiebant Spiritum Sanctum.

Actus 8:17

Ave Maria

Gloria Patri, et Filio, et Spiritui Sancto. Sicut
erat in principio, et nunc, et
semper, et in saecula
saeculorum.
Amen.

O mi Jesu, dimitte nobis debita nostra, libera
nos ab igne inferni, conduc in caelum omnes
animas, praesertim illas, quae
maxime indigent
misericordia
Tua.

Then they laid their hands upon them: and
they received the Holy Ghost.

Acts 8:17

Hail Mary

Glory be to the Father, and to the Son, and
to the Holy Spirit. As it was in the
beginning, is now, and
ever shall be. World
without end.
Amen.

O my Jesus, forgive us our sins, save
us from the fires of hell. Lead all
souls to heaven, especially
those who are most in
need of Thy
mercy.

Assumption of the
Virgin
Sano di Pietro (1406 - 1481)

The Assumption of the Virgin Mary

O Immaculate Virgin, mother of God, and mother of humanity, we believe with all the fervor of our faith in your triumphal Assumption both in body and in soul into heaven where you are acclaimed as Queen by all the choirs of angels and all the legions of saints; we unite with them to praise and bless the Lord who has exalted you above all other pure creatures and to offer you the tribute of our devotion and our love.

We are inspired by the certainty that your eyes, which wept over the earth crimsoned by the blood of Jesus, are yet turned toward this world racked by wars and persecutions, the oppression of the just and the weak. From the shadows of this vale of tears, we seek in your heavenly assistance, tender mercy, comfort for our aching hearts, and help in the trials of church and country.

We believe finally that in the glory where you reign, clothed with the sun and crowned with stars, you are, after Jesus, the joy and gladness of all the angels and the saints, and from this earth, over which we tread as pilgrims, comforted by our faith in the future resurrection, we look to you— our life, our sweetness, our hope; draw us onward with the sweetness of your voice, so that one day, after our exile, you may show us Jesus, the blessed fruit of your womb.

—Pope Saint Pius X (1835 - 1914)
Apostolic reign (1903 - 1914)

Quartum Mysterium Gloriosum

Assumptio
Mariae
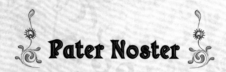

Fructus Mysterii: Gratia Beatae Mortis

Pater Noster

En dilectus meus loquitur mihi. Surge, propera,
amica mea, columba mea, formosa
mea, et veni. Canticum 2:10

Ave Maria

Quam pulchra es, amica
mea! Quam pulchra es … !

Canticum 4:1

Ave Maria

The Fourth Glorious Mystery

The Assumption
of Mary

Fruit of the Mystery: Grace of a Happy Death

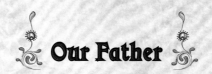

Behold, my beloved speaketh to me: Arise, make
haste, my love, my dove, my beautiful
one, and come. Song of Songs 2:10

How beautiful art thou, my love, how
beautiful art thou … !

Song of Songs 4:1

Tota pulchra es, amica mea, et
macula non est in te.
Canticum 4:7

Vulnerasti cor meum, soror mea,
sponsa; vulnerasti cor meum in uno oculorum
tuorum, et in uno crine colli
tui. Canticum 4:9

Hortus conclusus soror mea, sponsa, hortus
conclusus, fons signatus.

Canticum 4:12

… Viderunt eam filiae, et beatissimam
praedicaverunt; reginae et concubinae, et
laudaverunt eam. Canticum 6:8

Thou art all fair, O my love, and
there is not a spot in thee.
Song of Songs 4:7

 Hail Mary

Thou hast wounded my heart, my sister, my
spouse: thou hast wounded my heart with one
of thy eyes, and with one hair of thy
neck. Song of Songs 4:9

 Hail Mary

My sister, my spouse, is a garden enclosed, a
garden enclosed, a fountain sealed up.
Song of Songs 4:12

 Hail Mary

… The daughters saw her, and declared her
most blessed: the queens and concubines, and
they praised her. Song of Songs 6:8

 Hail Mary

Gaudens gaudebo in Domino, et exsultabit anima mea in Deo meo.

Isaias 61:10

 **Ave Maria**

Quia induit me vestimentis salutis, et indumento justitiae circumdedit me, quasi sponsum decoratum corona, et quasi sponsam ornatam monilibus suis. Isaias 61:10

 **Ave Maria**

Quam pulchra es, et quam decora, carissima, in deliciis!

Canticum 7:6

 **Ave Maria**

I will greatly rejoice in the Lord, and my
soul shall be joyful in my God.
Isaiah 61:10

 **Hail Mary**

For he hath clothed me with the garments of
salvation and with the robe of justice he hath covered
me: as a bridegroom decked with a crown and as a
bride adorned with her jewels. Isaiah 61:10

 **Hail Mary**

How beautiful art thou, and how
comely, my dearest, in delights!
Song of Songs 7:6

 **Hail Mary**

Memores erunt nominis tui in omni generatione
et generatione: propterea populi confitebuntur
tibi in aeternum, et in saeculum saeculi.
Psalmus 44:18

Ave Maria

Gloria Patri, et Filio, et Spiritui Sancto. Sicut
erat in principio, et nunc, et
semper, et in saecula
saeculorum.
Amen.

O mi Jesu, dimitte nobis debita nostra, libera
nos ab igne inferni, conduc in caelum
omnes animas, praesertim
illas, quae maxime indigent
misericordia Tua.

They shall remember thy name throughout all generations. Therefore shall people praise thee for ever: yea, for ever and ever.
Psalm 44:18

Hail Mary

Glory be to the Father, and to the Son, and
to the Holy Spirit. As it was in
the beginning, is now, and
ever shall be. World
without end.
Amen.

O my Jesus, forgive us our sins, save us
from the fires of hell. Lead all souls
to heaven, especially those who
are most in need of
Thy mercy.

The Queenship of the Virgin Mary

Hubert and Jan van Eyck
Ghent Altarpiece (1432)

Mary, Queen of Heaven

She [Mary] embellishes our works, adorning them with her own merits and virtues. It is as if a peasant, wishing to gain the friendship and benevolence of the king, went to the queen and presented her with a fruit which was his whole revenue, in order that she might present it to the king. The queen, having accepted the poor little offering from the peasant, would place the fruit on a large and beautiful dish of gold, and so, on the peasant's behalf, would present it to the king. Then the fruit, however unworthy in itself to be a king's present, would be worthy of his majesty because of the dish of gold on which it rested and the person who presented it.

She presents these good works to Jesus Christ; for she keeps nothing of what is given her for herself, as if she were our last end. She faithfully passes it all on to Jesus. If we give to her, we give necessarily to Jesus.

—Saint Louis De Montfort (1673 - 1716)

Quintum Mysterium Gloriosum

Coronatio
Mariae

Fructus Mysterii: Confidentia
Intercessionis Mariae

Pater Noster

... Et surrexit rex in occursum ejus, adoravitque
eam, et sedit super thronum suum: Positus quoque
est thronus matri regis, quae sedit ad dexteram ejus.

1 Regum 2:19

Ave Maria

Dixitque ei: Petitionem unam parvulam ego
deprecor a te, ne confundas faciem meam. Et
dixit ei rex: Pete, mater mea: neque enim fas
est ut avertam faciem tuam. *1 Regum 2:20*

Ave Maria

The Fifth Glorious Mystery

The Coronation  of Mary

Fruit of the Mystery: Trust in Mary's Intercession

 Our Father

… And the king rose to meet her, and bowed down to her; then he sat on his throne, and had a seat brought for the king's mother; and she sat on his right.

1 Kings 2:19

 Hail Mary

Then she said: I have one small request to make of you; do not refuse me. And the king said to her: Make your request, my mother; for I will not refuse you. 1 Kings 2:20

 **Hail Mary**

217

Quae cum exiisset ad illum, benedixerunt eam omnes una voce, dicentes: Tu gloria Jerusalem; tu laetitia Israel; tu honorificentia populi nostri. Judith 15:10

Et apertum est templum Dei in caelo: et visa est arca testamenti ejus in templo ejus. ... Apocalypsis 11:19

Et signum magnum apparuit in caelo: mulier amicta sole, et luna sub pedibus ejus, et in capite ejus corona stellarum duodecim. Apocalypsis 12:1

And when she was come out to him, they all blessed her with one voice, saying: Thou art the glory of Jerusalem, thou art the joy of Israel, thou art the honour of our people. Judith 15:10

And the temple of God was opened in heaven: and the ark of his testament was seen in his temple. ... Revelation 11:19

And a great sign appeared in heaven: A woman clothed with the sun, and the moon under her feet, and on her head a crown of twelve stars. Revelation 12:1

Et peperit filium masculum, qui recturus erat omnes gentes in virga ferrea: et raptus est filius ejus ad Deum, et ad thronum ejus. Apocalypsis 12:5

Astitit regina a dextris tuis in vestitu deaurato. ... Et concupiscet rex decorem tuum. Psalmus 44:10,12

Quae est ista quae progreditur quasi aurora consurgens, pulchra ut luna, electa ut sol, terribilis ut castrorum acies ordinata? Canticum 6:9

And she brought forth a man child, who was to
rule all nations with an iron rod. And her
son was taken up to God and to
his throne. Revelation 12:5

Hail Mary

The queen stood on thy right hand, in gilded
clothing. ... And the king shall greatly
desire thy beauty. Psalm 44:10,12

Hail Mary

Who is she that cometh forth as the morning
rising, fair as the moon, bright as the
sun, terrible as an army set
in array? Song of Songs 6:9

Hail Mary

Ego flos campi, et lilium convallium. Sicut
lilium inter spinas … . Canticum 2:1,2

Gloriosa dicta sunt de te, civitas Dei!
Psalmus 86:3

Gloria Patri, et Filio, et Spiritui Sancto. Sicut
erat in principio, et nunc, et
semper, et in saecula
saeculorum.
Amen.

O mi Jesu, dimitte nobis debita nostra, libera
nos ab igne inferni, conduc in caelum
omnes animas, praesertim
illas, quae maxime indigent
misericordia Tua.

I am the flower of the field, and the lily of the valleys. As a lily among thorns .... Song of Songs 2:1,2

Hail Mary

Glorious things are said of thee: O city of God.

Psalm 86:3

Hail Mary

Glory be to the Father, and to the Son, and
to the Holy Spirit. As it was in the
beginning, is now, and
ever shall be. World
without end.
Amen.

O my Jesus, forgive us our sins, save us
from the fires of hell. Lead all souls
to heaven, especially those who
are most in need of
Thy mercy.

The Luminous
Mysteries

The Baptism of Christ
Annibale Carracci (1560 - 1609)

The Baptism of Jesus

he act of descending into the waters of this Baptism implies a confession of guilt and a plea for forgiveness in order to make a new beginning. In a world marked by sin, then, this Yes to the entire will of God also expresses solidarity with men, who have incurred guilt but yearn for righteousness. The significance of this event could not fully emerge until it was seen in light of the Cross and Resurrection. Descending into the water, the candidates for Baptism confess their sin and seek to be rid of their burden of guilt. What did Jesus do in the same situation? Luke, who throughout his Gospel is keenly attentive to Jesus' prayer, and portrays Him again and again at prayer— in conversation with the Father— tells that Jesus was praying while He received Baptism (cf. Lk 3:21). Looking at the events in light of the Cross and Resurrection, the Christian people realize what happened: Jesus loaded the burden of all mankind's guilt upon His shoulders; He bore it down into the depths of the Jordan. He inaugurated His public activity by stepping into the place of sinners.

His inaugural gesture is an anticipation of the Cross. He is, as it were, the true Jonah who said to the crew of the ship, "Take me and throw me into the sea" (Jon 1:12). The whole significance of Jesus' Baptism, the fact that He bears "all righteousness" first comes to light on the Cross: The Baptism is an acceptance of death for the sins of humanity, and the voice that calls out "This is my beloved Son" over the baptismal waters is an anticipatory reference to the Resurrection. This also explains why, in His own discourses, Jesus uses the word baptism to refer to His death (cf. Mk 10:38; Lk 12:50).

—Pope Benedict XVI (1927 -)
Apostolic reign (2005 - 2013)

Primum Mysterium Luminosum

Baptisma Jesu
 # in Jordane

Fructus Mysterii: Ut Aperiamur
Spiritui Sancto

 ## Pater Noster

Naaman princeps militiae regis Syriae, erat vir
magnus apud dominum suum, et honoratus ...
erat autem vir fortis et dives, sed
leprosus. 2 Regum 5:1

 ## Ave Maria

Dixitque ei rex Syriae: Vade, et mittam litteras
ad regem Israel. ... Detulit litteras ad regem
Israel, in haec verba: Cum acceperis epistolam
hanc, scito quod miserim ad te Naaman
servum meum, ut cures eum a lepra sua.

2 Regum 5:5,6

 ## Ave Maria

The First Luminous Mystery

The Baptism of Jesus in the Jordan

Fruit of the Mystery: Openness
to the Holy Spirit

Our Father

Naaman, commander of the army of the king of
Syria, was a great man with his master and in high
favor. ... He was a mighty man of valor,
but he was a leper. 2 Kings 5:1 (R.S.V.)

Hail Mary

And the king of Syria said: Go now, and I will send a
letter to the king of Israel. ... And he brought the letter
to the king of Israel, which read: When this letter
reaches you, know that I have sent to you Naaman
my servant, that you may cure him of his leprosy.

2 Kings 5:5,6 (R.S.V.)

Hail Mary

Cumque legisset rex Israel litteras, scidit vestimenta sua, et ait: Numquid Deus ego sum, ut occidere possim et vivificare, ut curem hominem a lepra sua? ... 2 Regum 5:7

Quod cum audisset Eliseus vir Dei, scidisse videlicet, regem Israel vestimenta sua misit ad eum, dicens ... Veniat ad me et sciat esse prophetam in Israel. 2 Regum 5:8

Misitque ad eum Eliseus nuntium, dicens: Vade, et lavare septies in Jordane, et recipiet sanitatem caro tua, atque mundaberis. ... Descendit, et lavit in Jordane septies, et restituta est caro ejus, sicut caro pueri parvuli, et mundatus est. 2 Regum 5;10,14

And when the king of Israel had read the letter, he rent his garments, and said: Am I God, to be able to kill and give life, to heal a man of his leprosy? ... 4 Kings 5:7

Hail Mary

And when Eliseus the man of God had heard that the king of Israel had rent his garments, he sent to him, saying ... Let him come to me; and let him know that there is a prophet in Israel. 4 Kings 5:8

Hail Mary

And Eliseus sent a messenger to him, saying: Go and wash seven times in the Jordan; and thy flesh shall recover health; and thou shall be clean. ... Then he went down, and washed in the Jordan seven times. And his flesh was restored, like the flesh of a little child: and he was made clean. 4 Kings 5;10,14

Hail Mary

... Amen, amen dico tibi, nisi quis renatus fuerit ex aqua, et Spiritu Sancto, non potest introire in regnum Dei. Joannes 3:5

Ave Maria

Fuit Joannes in deserto baptizans, et praedicans baptismum poenitentiae in remissionem peccatorum. ... Et praedicabat dicens: Venit fortior post me, cujus non sum dignus procumbens solvere corrigiam calceamentorum ejus. Marcus 1:4,7

Ave Maria

Ego quidem baptizo vos in aqua in poenitentiam: qui autem post me venturus est, fortior me est ... . Ipse vos baptizabit in Spiritu Sancto, et igni. Matthaeus 3:11

Ave Maria

... Amen, amen, I say to thee, unless a man be born again of water and the Holy Ghost, he cannot enter into the kingdom of God. John 3:5

Hail Mary

John was in the desert baptizing, and preaching the baptism of penance, unto remission of sins. ... And he preached, saying: There cometh after me one mightier than I, the latchet of whose shoes I am not worthy to stoop down and loose. Mark 1:4,7

Hail Mary

I indeed baptize you in water unto penance: but he that shall come after me is mightier than I ... . He shall baptize you in the Holy Ghost and fire. Matthew 3:11

Hail Mary

Tunc venit Jesus a Galilaea in Jordanem ad Joannem, ut baptizaretur ab eo. Joannes autem prohibebat eum, dicens: Ego a te debeo baptizari, et tu venis ad me? Matthaeus 3:13,14

Ave Maria

Baptizatus autem Jesus, confestim ascendit de aqua, et ecce aperti sunt ei caeli: et vidit Spiritum Dei descendentem sicut columbam, et venientem super se. Et ecce vox de caelis dicens: Hic est Filius meus dilectus, in quo mihi complacui. Matthaeus 3:16,17

Ave Maria

Gloria Patri, et Filio, et Spiritui Sancto. Sicut erat in principio, et nunc, et semper, et in saecula saeculorum.
Amen.

O mi Jesu, dimitte nobis debita nostra, libera nos ab igne inferni, conduc in caelum omnes animas, praesertim illas, quae maxime indigent misericordia Tua.

Then cometh Jesus from Galilee to the Jordan, unto John, to be baptized by him. But John stayed him, saying: I ought to be baptized by thee, and comest thou to me? Matthew 3:13,14

Hail Mary

And Jesus being baptized, forthwith came out of the water: and lo, the heavens were opened to him: and he saw the Spirit of God descending as a dove and coming upon him. And behold a voice from heaven, saying: This is my beloved Son, in whom I am well pleased. Matthew 3:16,17

Hail Mary

Glory be to the Father, and to the Son, and to the Holy Spirit. As it was in the beginning, is now, and ever shall be. World without end. Amen.

O my Jesus, forgive us our sins, save us from the fires of hell. Lead all souls to heaven, especially those who are most in need of Thy mercy.

237

The Marriage Feast at Cana
Juan de Flandes (1460 - 1519)

The Sacrament of Marriage

he marriage of those who have been baptized is…invested with the dignity of a sacramental sign of grace, for it represents the union of Christ and His Church. …

This love is above all fully human, a compound of sense and spirit. It is not, then, merely a question of natural instinct or emotional drive. It is also, and above all, an act of the free will, whose trust is such that it is meant not only to survive the joys and sorrows of daily life, but also to grow, so that husband and wife become in a way one heart and one soul, and together attain their human fulfillment.

It is a love which is total—that very special form of personal friendship in which husband and wife generously share everything, allowing no unreasonable exceptions and not thinking solely of their own convenience. Whoever really

loves his partner loves not only for what he receives, but loves that partner for the partner's own sake, content to be able to enrich the other with the gift of himself.

Married love is also faithful and exclusive of all others, and this until death. ...

Finally, this love is fecund. It is not confined wholly to the loving interchange of husband and wife; it also contrives to go beyond this to bring new life into being. Marriage and conjugal love are by their nature ordained toward the procreation and education of children. Children are really the supreme gift of marriage and contribute in the highest degree to their parents' welfare. ...

—Blessed Pope Paul VI (1897 - 1978)
Apostolic reign (1963 - 1978)

Secundum Mysterium Luminosum

Nuptiae in

Cana

Fructus Mysterii: Ad Jesum per Mariam

Pater Noster

Et erit in die illa, ait Dominus: vocabit me, Vir
meus. ... Et sponsabo te mihi in
sempiternum. Osee 2:16,19

Ave Maria

Non vocaberis ultra Derelicta, et terra tua non
vocabitur amplius Desolata; sed vocaberis
Voluntas mea in ea, et terra tua
Inhabitata. Isaias 62:4

Ave Maria

The Second Luminous Mystery

The Wedding Feast

At Cana

Fruit of the Mystery: To Jesus Through Mary

Our Father

And it shall be in that day, saith the Lord, that she shall call me, My husband. ... And I will espouse thee to me for ever. Hosea 2:16,19

Hail Mary

Thou shalt no more be called Forsaken, and thy land shall no more be called Desolate: but thou shalt be called My pleasure in her, and thy land Inhabited. Isaiah 62:4

Hail Mary

Et dicam Non populo meo; Populus
meus es tu; et ipse dicet: Deus
meus es tu. Osee 2:24

Et die tertia nuptiae factae sunt in Cana
Galilaeae, et erat mater Jesu ibi. Vocatus est
autem et Jesus, et discipuli ejus, ad
nuptias. Joannes 2:1,2

… Et deficiente vino, dicit mater Jesu ad eum:
Vinum non habent. Et dicit ei Jesus: Quid mihi et tibi
est, mulier? Nondum venit hora mea. Dicit mater
ejus ministris: Quodcumque dixerit
vobis, facite. Joannes 2:3-5

And I will say to that which was not my people:
Thou art my people. And they
shall say: Thou art my God. Hosea 2:24

There was a marriage in Cana of Galilee: and
the mother of Jesus was there. Jesus
also was invited, and his disciples, to
the marriage. John 2:1,2

... And the wine failing, the mother of Jesus saith to
him: They have no wine. And Jesus saith to her:
Woman, what is that to me and to thee: My hour is
not yet come. His mother saith to the waiters:
Whatsoever he shall say to you, do ye. John 2:3-5

Dicit eis Jesus: Implete hydrias aqua. Et impleverunt eas usque ad summum. Et dicit eis Jesus: Haurite nunc, et ferte architriclino. Et tulerunt. Joannes 2:7,8

Ave Maria

Ut autem gustavit architriclinus aquam vinum factam, et non sciebat unde esset, ministri autem sciebant, qui hauserant aquam: vocat sponsum architriclinus, et dicit ei: Omnis homo primum bonum vinum ponit et cum inebriati fuerint, tunc id, quod deterius est. Tu autem servasti bonum vinum usque adhuc. Joannes 2:9,10

Ave Maria

Viri, diligite uxores vestras, sicut et Christus dilexit Ecclesiam, et seipsum tradidit pro ea, ut illam sanctificaret, mundans lavacro aquae in verbo vitae. Ephesios 5:25,26

Ave Maria

Jesus saith to them: Fill the waterpots with water. And they filled them up to the brim. And Jesus saith to them: Draw out now and carry to the chief steward of the feast. And they carried it. John 2:7,8

And when the chief steward had tasted the water made wine and knew not whence it was, the chief steward calleth the bridegroom, and saith to him: Every man at first setteth forth good wine, and when men have well drunk, then that which is worse. But thou has kept the good wine until now. John 2:9,10

Husbands, love your wives, as Christ loved the church and gave himself up for her, that he might sanctify her, having cleansed her by the washing of water with the word. Ephesians 5:25,26

Ut exhiberet ipse sibi gloriosam Ecclesiam, non habentem maculam, aut rugam, aut aliquid hujusmodi, sed ut sit sancta et immaculata. Ephesios 5:27

Ave Maria

Et erunt duo in carne una. Itaque jam non sunt duo, sed una caro. Quod ergo Deus conjunxit, homo non separet. Marcus 10:8,9

Ave Maria

Gloria Patri, et Filio, et Spiritui Sancto. Sicut erat in principio, et nunc, et semper, et in saecula saeculorum.
Amen

O mi Jesu, dimitte nobis debita nostra, libera nos ab igne inferni, conduc in caelum omnes animas, praesertim illas, quae maxime indigent misericordia Tua.

That he might present the church to himself in splendor, without spot or wrinkle or any such thing, that she might be holy and without blemish. Ephesians 5:27

Hail Mary

And they two shall be in one flesh. Therefore now they are not two, but one flesh. What therefore God hath joined together, let no man put asunder. Mark 10:8,9

Hail Mary

Glory be to the Father, and to the Son, and to the Holy Spirit. As it was in the beginning, is now, and ever shall be. World without end. Amen.

O my Jesus, forgive us our sins, save us from the fires of hell. Lead all souls to heaven, especially those who are most in need of Thy mercy.

The Storm on the
Sea of Galilee

Rembrandt
(1606 - 1669)

The Barque of Peter

The Church upon earth, consists of millions of souls at various stages on the road that leads to sanctity. Some have attained it but must still struggle to remain in it; some are close to it, some not so close, some seem to have given up the struggle, some even seem to be headed viciously away from it. That is the reality of the human society at any given time. It is made up, in a proportion that changes from moment to moment, of men headed for heaven, men headed for hell, and men apparently not headed anywhere. And it is through *this* society that Christ is operating.

He guarantees that the truth and the life and the unity shall not fail. But He fulfills His guarantee without doing violence either to the nature of man or to the nature of human society. Having chosen to act upon men through a society of men, Christ is faithful to the logic of his choice. The men remain men; the society remains a society of men. They do glorious things, they do horrible things.

It is the especial meaning of the Church that in it Our Lord unites men to Himself *through humanity*—not through some ideal humanity, but through the humanity, good, bad, and indifferent, that actually exists. As Matthew Arnold notes, where other religions suggest a special type of man, Catholics suggest "all the pell mell of the men and women of Shakespeare's plays." There is a special kind of spiritual man who finds all this intolerable. His every instinct is revolted at the thought of Christ's working in and through, and of himself being sanctified in and through, this mixed crowd of human beings. The hot smell of humanity is too strong for him. He would have his own direct relation with God, excluding the turbulence of humanity; or he would make his own choice of the men he feels God would choose. But this is preciousness and folly. It is as though the man Christ healed by the touch of His spittle had asked to be healed some other way—he was a refined man, perhaps, brought up to regard spittle as vulgar, or even unhygienic. One cannot be thus delicate about the gifts of God. ... We do not join the Church for the company, but for the gifts.

—Frank Sheed (1897 - 1981)

Proclamatio Regni

Fructus Mysterii: Poenitentia et Confidentia Dei

Pater Noster

Framea, suscitare super pastorem meum, et super virum cohaerentem mihi, dicit Dominus exercituum. Percute pastorem, et dispergentur oves: et convertam manum meam ad parvulos. Zacharias 13:7

Ave Maria

… Probabo eos sicut probatur aurum. Ipse vocabit nomen meum, et ego exaudiam eos. Dicam: Populus meus es: et ipse dicet: Dominus Deus meus. Zacharias 13:9

Ave Maria

The Third Luminous Mystery

The Proclamation of the Kingdom

Fruit of the Mystery: Repentance and Trust in God

Our Father

Awake, O sword, against my shepherd and against the man that cleaveth to me, saith the Lord of hosts. Strike the shepherd, and the sheep shall be scattered. And I will turn my hand to the little ones. Zechariah 13:7

Hail Mary

… And I will try them as gold is tried. They shall call on my name, and I will hear them. I will say: Thou art my people. And they shall say: The Lord is my God. Zechariah 13:9

Hail Mary

... Suscitabit Deus caeli regnum, quod in aeternum non dissipabitur, et regnum ejus alteri populo non tradetur: comminuet autem, et consumet universa regna haec, et ipsum stabit in aeternum. Daniel 2:44

Ave Maria

Sicut ergo colliguntur zizania, et igni comburuntur: sic erit in consummatione saeculi. Mittet Filius hominis angelos suos, et colligent de regno ejus omnia scandala, et eos qui faciunt iniquitatem. Et mittent eos in caminum ignis. ... Matthaeus 13:40-42

Ave Maria

Imple facies eorum ignominia, et quaerent nomen tuum, Domine. Erubescant, et conturbentur in saeculum saeculi, et confundantur, et pereant. Psalmus 82:17,18

Ave Maria

… The God of heaven will set up a kingdom that shall never be destroyed: and his kingdom shall not be delivered up to another people. And it shall break in pieces and shall consume all these kingdoms: And itself shall stand for ever. Daniel 2:44

Hail Mary

Just as the weeds are gathered and burned with fire, so will it be at the close of the age. The Son of man will send his angels, and they will gather out of his kingdom all causes of sin and all evildoers, and throw them into the furnace of fire. … Matthew 13:40-42

Hail Mary

Fill their faces with shame: and they shall seek thy name, O Lord. Let them be ashamed and troubled for ever and ever; and let them be confounded and perish. Psalm 82:17,18

Hail Mary

Ambulans autem Jesus juxta mare Galilaeae, vidit duos fratres, Simonem, qui vocatur Petrus, et Andream fratrem ejus, mittentes rete in mare …. Et ait illis: Venite post me, et faciam vos fieri piscatores hominum. At illi continuo relictis retibus secuti sunt eum. Matthaeus 4:18-20

Respondit ergo ei Simon Petrus … Nos credidimus, et cognovimus quia tu es Christus Filius Dei. Respondit eis Jesus: Nonne ego vos duodecim elegi: et ex vobis unus diabolus est? Joannes 6:69-71

Sciebat enim quisnam esset qui traderet eum; propterea dixit: Non estis mundi omnes. Joannes 13:11

And Jesus walking by the sea of Galilee, saw two brethren, Simon who is called Peter and Andrew his brother, casting a net into the sea .... And he saith to them: Come ye after me, and I will make you to be fishers of men. And they immediately leaving their nets, followed him. Matthew 4:18-20

Hail Mary

Simon Peter answered him ... We have believed and have known that thou art the Christ the Son of God. Jesus answered them: Have not I chosen you twelve? And one of you is a devil. John 6:69-71

Hail Mary

For he knew who he was that would betray him; therefore he said: You are not all clean. John 13:11

Hail Mary

Et ego dico tibi, quia tu es Petrus, et super hanc
petram aedificabo Ecclesiam meam, et
portae inferi non praevalebunt
adversus eam. Matthaeus 16:18

 Ave Maria

Misericordia et veritas te non deserant; circumda eas
gutturi tuo, et describe in tabulis cordis tui. ... Habe
fiduciam in Domino ex toto corde tuo, et ne innitaris
prudentiae tuae. In omnibus viis tuis cogita
illum, et ipse diriget gressus tuos.
Proverbia 3:3,5,6

 Ave Maria

Gloria Patri, et Filio, et Spiritui Sancto. Sicut
erat in principio, et nunc, et
semper, et in saecula
saeculorum.
Amen.

O mi Jesu, dimitte nobis debita nostra, libera
nos ab igne inferni, conduc in caelum omnes
animas, praesertim illas, quae maxime indigent
misericordia Tua.

And I say to thee: That thou art Peter, and
upon this rock I will build my church. And
the gates of hell shall not prevail
against it. Matthew 16:18

Hail Mary

Let not mercy and truth leave thee. Put them about
thy neck, and write them in the tablets of thy heart. ...
Have confidence in the Lord with all thy heart, and lean
not on thy own prudence. In all thy ways think
on him: and he will direct thy steps.
Proverbs 3:3,5,6

Hail Mary

Glory be to the Father, and to the Son, and
to the Holy Spirit. As it was in the
beginning, is now, and ever shall
be. World without end.
Amen.

O my Jesus, forgive us our sins, save us
from the fires of hell. Lead all souls to heaven,
especially those who are most
in need of Thy mercy.

DOMINE BONVM EST NOS HIC ESSE

The Transfiguration
Perugino (1446/1450 - 1523)

The Divinity of Jesus Made Manifest to His Chosen Apostles

In this Transfiguration the foremost object was to remove the offence of the cross from the disciples' hearts, and to prevent their faith being disturbed by the humiliation of His voluntary Passion by revealing to them the excellence of His hidden dignity.

And so while He was yet speaking, behold a bright cloud overshadowed them, and behold a voice out of the cloud, saying, "This is My beloved Son, in whom I am well pleased; hear ye Him." The Father was indeed present in the Son, and in the Lord's brightness, which He had tempered to the disciples' sight, the Father's Essence was not separated from the Only-begotten: but, in order to emphasize the two-fold personality, as the effulgence of the Son's body displayed the Son to their sight, so the Father's voice from out of the cloud announced the Father to their hearing. And when this voice was heard, "the disciples fell upon their faces, and were sore afraid," trembling at the majesty, not only of the Father, but also of the Son: for they now had a deeper insight into the undivided Deity of Both: and in their fear they did not separate the One from the Other, because they doubted not in their faith. That was a wide and manifold testimony, therefore, and contained a fuller meaning than struck the ear. For when the Father said, "This is My beloved Son ..." was it not clearly meant, "This is My Son," Whose it is to be eternally from Me and with Me? Because the Begetter is not anterior to the Begotten, nor the Begotten posterior to the Begetter. "This is My Son," Who is separated from Me, neither by Godhead, nor by power, nor by eternity.

"This is My Son," not adopted, but true-born, not created from another source, but begotten of Me: nor yet made like Me from another nature, but born equal to Me of My nature.

"This is My Son," through Whom all things were made, and without Whom was nothing made because all things that I do He does in like manner: and whatever I perform, He performs with Me inseparably and without difference: for the Son is in the Father and the Father in the Son, and Our Unity is never divided: and though I am One Who begot, and He the Other Whom I begot, yet it is wrong for you to think anything of Him which is not possible of Me.

"This is My Son," Who sought not by grasping, and seized not in greediness, that equality with Me which He has, but remaining in the form of My glory, that He might carry out Our common plan for the restoration of mankind, He lowered the unchangeable Godhead even to the form of a slave.

... Let all men's faith then be established, according to the preaching of the holy Gospel, and let no one be ashamed of Christ's Cross, through which the world was redeemed. And let not anyone fear to suffer for righteousness' sake, or doubt of the fulfillment of the promises, for this reason, that through toil we pass to rest and through death to life; since all the weakness of our lowly human nature was assumed by Him, in Whom, if we abide in the acknowledgement and love of Him, we conquer as He conquered, and receive what He promised, because, whether to the performance of His commands or to the endurance of adversities, the Father's fore-announcing voice should always be sounding in our ears, saying, "This is My beloved Son, in Whom I am well pleased; hear ye Him": Who liveth and reigneth, with the Father and the Holy Ghost, for ever and ever. Amen.

—Pope Saint Leo the Great (unknown - 461)
Apostolic reign 440 - 461

Quartum Mysterium Luminosum

 Transfiguratio

Fructus Mysterii: Desiderium Sanctitatis

Pater Noster

… Qui credit in me, non credit in me, sed in eum
qui misit me. Et qui videt me, videt eum
qui misit me. Joannes 12:44,45

Ave Maria

Et Super firmamentum, quod erat imminens
capiti eorum, quasi aspectus lapidis sapphiri
similitudo throni: et super similitudinem
throni similitudo quasi aspectus
hominis desuper. Ezechiel 1:26

Ave Maria

The Fourth Luminous Mystery

 # The Transfiguration

The Fruit of the Mystery: Desire for Holiness

Our Father

… He that believeth in me doth not believe in me, but in him that sent me. And he that seeth me, seeth him that sent me. John 12:44,45

Hail Mary

And above the firmament over their heads there was the likeness of a throne, in appearance like sapphire; and seated above the likeness of a throne was a likeness as it were of a human form. Ezekiel 1:26

Hail Mary

Dixit eis Jesus: Amen, amen dico vobis, antequam Abraham fieret, ego sum. ... Qui videt me, videt et Patrem. ... Joannes 8:58; 14:9

 **Ave Maria**

Factum est autem ... et assumpsit Petrum, et Jacobum, et Joannem, et ascendit in montem ut oraret. Lucas 9:28

 **Ave Maria**

Et transfiguratus est ante eos. Et resplenduit facies ejus sicut sol: vestimenta autem ejus facta sunt alba sicut nix. Matthaeus 17:2

 **Ave Maria**

Et ecce duo viri loquebantur cum illo. Erant autem Moyses et Elias, visi in majestate: et dicebant excessum ejus, quem completurus erat in Jerusalem. Lucas 9:30,31

 **Ave Maria**

Jesus said to them: Amen, amen, I say to you, before Abraham was made, I AM. ... He that seeth me seeth the Father also. ... John 8:58; 14:9

Hail Mary

And it came to pass ... that he took Peter, and James, and John, and went up into a mountain to pray. Luke 9:28

Hail Mary

He was transfigured before them. And his face did shine as the sun: and his garments became white as snow. Matthew 17:2

Hail Mary

And behold two men were talking with him. They were Moses and Elias, appearing in majesty. And they spoke of his decease that he should accomplish in Jerusalem. Luke 9:30,31

Hail Mary

Petrus vero, et qui cum illo erant, gravati erant somno. Et evigilantes viderunt majestatem ejus, et duos viros qui stabant cum illo. Et factum est cum discederent ab illo, ait Petrus ad Jesum: Praeceptor, bonum est nos hic esse … . Lucas 9:32,33

 **Ave Maria**

Haec autem illo loquente, facta est nubes, et obumbravit eos: et timuerunt, intrantibus illis in nubem. Et vox facta est de nube, dicens: Hic est Filius meus dilectus, ipsum audite. Lucas 9:34,35

 **Ave Maria**

Et audientes discipuli ceciderunt in faciem suam, et timuerunt valde.

Matthaeus 17:6

 **Ave Maria**

But Peter and they that were with him were heavy
with sleep. And waking, they saw his glory, and the
two men that stood with him. And it came to pass
that, as they were departing from him, Peter
saith to Jesus: Master, it is good for us
to be here .... Luke 9:32,33

And as he spoke these things, there came a cloud
and overshadowed them. And they were afraid
when they entered the cloud. And a voice
came out of the cloud, saying: This is my
beloved Son: Hear him. Luke 9:34,35

And the disciples hearing, fell upon their
face and were very much afraid.

Matthew 17:6

273

Et accessit Jesus, et tetigit eos: dixitque eis:
Surgite, et nolite timere. Levantes autem
oculos suos, neminem viderunt, nisi
solum Jesum. Matthaeus 17:7,8

Ave Maria

Gloria Patri, et Filio, et Spiritui Sancto. Sicut
erat in principio, et nunc, et
semper, et in saecula
saeculorum.
Amen

O mi Jesu, dimitte nobis debita nostra, libera
nos ab igne inferni, conduc in caelum
omnes animas, praesertim
illas, quae maxime indigent
misericordia Tua.

And Jesus came and touched them and said
to them: Arise, and fear not. And they
lifting up their eyes saw no one but
only Jesus. Matthew 17:7,8

Hail Mary

Glory be to the Father, and to the Son, and
to the Holy Spirit. As it was in
the beginning, is now, and
ever shall be. World
without end.
Amen.

O my Jesus, forgive us our sins, save us from
the fires of hell. Lead all souls to heaven,
especially those who are most
in need of Thy
mercy.

Supper at Emmaus
Titian (1488/90 - 1576)

The Eucharist:
The Source and Summit
of the Christian Life

he Church draws her life from the Eucharist. This truth does not simply express a daily experience of faith, but recapitulates the heart of the mystery of the Church. In a variety of ways she joyfully experiences the constant fulfillment of the promise: "Lo, I am with you always, to the close of the age" (Mt 28:20), but in the Holy Eucharist through the changing of the bread and wine into the body and blood of the Lord, she rejoices in this presence with unique intensity. ...

The Second Vatican Council rightly proclaimed that the Eucharistic sacrifice is "the source and summit of the Christian life." "For the most holy Eucharist contains the Church's entire spiritual wealth: Christ Himself, our passover and living bread. Through His own flesh, now made living and life-giving by the Holy Spirit, He offers life to men." Consequently the gaze of the Church is constantly turned to her Lord, present in the Sacrament of the Altar, in which she discovers the full manifestation of His boundless love. ...

The Church draws her life from Christ in the Eucharist; by Him she is fed and by Him she is enlightened. ... Whenever the Church celebrates the Eucharist, the faithful can in some way relive the experience of the two disciples on the road to Emmaus: "their eyes were opened and they recognized Him" (Lk 24:31). ...

... [The Eucharist] unites heaven and earth. It embraces and permeates all creation. The Son of God became man in order to restore all creation, in one supreme act of praise, to the One who made it from nothing. He, the Eternal High Priest who by the blood of His Cross entered the eternal sanctuary, thus gives back to the Creator and Father all creation redeemed. He does so through the priestly ministry of the Church, to the glory of the Most Holy Trinity. Truly this is the *mysterium fidei* which is accomplished in the Eucharist: the world which came forth from the hands of God the Creator now returns to Him redeemed by Christ.

The Eucharist, as Christ's saving presence in the community of the faithful and its spiritual food, is the most precious possession which the Church can have in her journey through history. ...

The Church has received the Eucharist from Christ her Lord not as one gift—however precious—among many others, but as the gift *par excellence*, for it is the gift of Himself, of His person in His sacred humanity, as well as the gift of His saving work. Nor does it remain confined to the past, since "all that Christ is—all that He did and suffered for all men—participates in the divine eternity, and so transcends all time."

When the Church celebrates the Eucharist, the memorial of her Lord's death and Resurrection, this central event of salvation becomes really present and "the work of our redemption is carried out." This sacrifice is so decisive for the salvation of the human race that Jesus Christ offered it and returned to the Father only after He had left us a means of sharing in it as if we had been present there. Each member of the faithful can thus take part in it and inexhaustibly gain its fruits. This is the faith which generations of Christians down the ages have lived. The Church's Magisterium has consistently reaffirmed this faith with joyful gratitude for its inestimable gift. ... What more could Jesus have done for us? Truly, in the Eucharist, He shows us a love which goes "to the end" (cf. Jn 13:1), a love which knows no measure. ...

The Mass makes present the sacrifice of the Cross; it does not add to that sacrifice nor does it multiply it. What is repeated is its memorial celebration, its "commemorative representation," which makes Christ's one definitive redemptive sacrifice always present in time. The sacrificial nature of the Eucharistic mystery cannot therefore be understood as something separate, independent of the Cross or only indirectly referring to the sacrifice of Calvary. ...

... The consecration of the bread and wine effects the change of the whole substance of the bread into the substance of the body of Christ our Lord, and of the whole substance of the wine into the substance of His blood. ... "Do not see"— Saint Cyril of Jerusalem exhorts— "in the bread and wine merely natural elements, because the Lord has expressly said that they are His body and His blood: faith assures you of this, though your senses suggest otherwise." ...

When for the first time Jesus spoke of this food, His listeners were astonished and bewildered, which forced the Master to emphasize the objective truth of His words: "Truly, truly I say to you, unless you eat the flesh of the Son of Man and drink His blood, you have no life within you" (Jn 6:53). This is no metaphorical food: "My flesh is food indeed, and My blood is drink indeed" (Jn 6:55). ...

"He who eats My flesh and drinks My blood has eternal life, and I will raise him up on the last day" (Jn 6:54). This pledge of the future resurrection comes from the fact that the flesh of the Son of Man, given as food, is His body in its glorious state after the Resurrection. With the Eucharist we digest, as it were, the "secret" of the Resurrection. For this reason Saint Ignatius of Antioch rightly defined the Eucharistic Bread as "a medicine of immortality, an antidote to death." ...

A great and transcendent mystery, indeed, and one that taxes our mind's ability to pass beyond appearances. Here our senses fail us. Yet faith alone, rooted in the word of Christ handed down to us by the Apostles, is sufficient for us. Allow me, like Peter at the end of the Eucharistic discourse in John's Gospel, to say once more to Christ, in the name of the whole Church and in the name of each of you: "Lord, to whom shall we go? You have the words of eternal life" (Jn 6:68). ...

By giving the Eucharist the prominence it deserves, and by being careful not to diminish any of its dimensions or demands, we show that we are truly conscious of the greatness of this gift. We are urged to do so by an uninterrupted tradition, which from the first centuries on has found the Christian community ever vigilant guarding this "treasure." Inspired by love, the Church is anxious to hand on to future generations of Christians, without loss, her faith and teaching with regard to the mystery of the

282

Eucharist. There can be no danger of excess in our care for this mystery, for "in this sacrament is recapitulated the whole mystery of our salvation."

—Pope Saint John Paul II (1920 - 2005)
Apostolic reign (1978 - 2005)

Quintum Mysterium Luminosum

Institutio Eucharistiae

Fructus Mysterii: Adoratio Eucharistiae

Pater Noster

Dixit autem Dominus ad Moysen: Ecce ego pluam vobis panes de caelo: egrediatur populus, et colligat quae sufficiunt per singulos dies … . Exodus 16:4

Ave Maria

Et mandavit nubibus desuper, et januas caeli aperuit. Et pluit illis manna ad manducandum, et panem caeli dedit eis. Psalmus 77:23,24

Ave Maria

The Fifth Luminous Mystery

The Institution of the Eucharist

Fruit of the Mystery: Eucharistic Adoration

Our Father

And the Lord said to Moses: Behold I will rain
bread from heaven for you. Let the people
go forth, and gather what is sufficient
for every day .... Exodus 16:4

Hail Mary

And he had commanded the clouds from above: and
had opened the doors of heaven. And had rained down
manna upon them to eat: and had given them
the bread of heaven. Psalm 77:23,24

Hail Mary

… Pro quibus angelorum esca nutrivisti populum tuum; et paratum panem de caelo praestitisti illis sine labore, omne delectamentum in se habentem, et omnis saporis suavitatem. Sapientia 16:20

Ego sum panis vivus, qui de caelo descendi. Si quis manducaverit ex hoc pane, vivet in aeternum …. Caro enim mea vere est cibus: et sanguis meus, vere est potus. Joannes 6:51,52,56

Multi ergo audientes ex discipulis ejus, dixerunt: Durus est hic sermo, et quis potest eum audire? Sciens autem Jesus apud semetipsum quia murmurarent de hoc discipuli ejus, dixit eis: Hoc vos scandalizat?… Sed sunt quidam ex vobis qui non credunt. Joannes 6:61,62,65

... Thou didst feed thy people with the food of angels, and gavest them bread from heaven, prepared without labour; having in it all that is delicious and the sweetness of every taste. Wisdom 16:20

Hail Mary

I am the living bread which came down from heaven. If any man eat of this bread, he shall live for ever ... . For my flesh is meat indeed: and my blood is drink indeed. John 6:51,52,56

Hail Mary

Many therefore, of his disciples, hearing it, said: This saying is hard; and who can hear it? But Jesus, knowing in himself that his disciples murmured at this, said to them: Doth this scandalize you?... But there are some of you that believe not. John 6:61,62,65

Hail Mary

Ex hoc multi discipulorum ejus abierunt retro: et jam non cum illo ambulabant. Dixit ergo Jesus ad duodecim: Numquid et vos vultis abire? Respondit ergo ei Simon Petrus: Domine, ad quem ibimus? Verba vitae aeternae habes. Joannes 6:67-69

Ave Maria

Coenantibus autem eis, accepit Jesus panem, et benedixit, ac fregit, deditque discipulis suis, et ait: Accipite, et comedite: hoc est corpus meum. Et accipiens calicem, gratias egit: et dedit illis, dicens: Bibite ex hoc omnes. Hic est enim sanguis meus novi testamenti, qui pro multis effundetur in remissionem peccatorum. Matthaeus 26:26-28

Ave Maria

After this, many of his disciples went back and walked no more with him. Then Jesus said to the twelve: Will you also go away? And Simon Peter answered him: Lord, to whom shall we go? Thou has the words of eternal life. John 6:67-69

Hail Mary

Now as they were eating, Jesus took bread, and blessed, and broke it, and gave it to the disciples and said: Take, eat; this is my body. And he took a chalice, and when he had given thanks he gave it to them, saying: Drink of it, all of you; for this is my blood of the covenant, which is poured out for many for the forgiveness of sins. Matthew 26:26-28

Hail Mary

… Duo ex illis ibant ipsa die in castellum … nomine
Emmaus. Et ipse Jesus appropinquans
ibat cum illis. … Et appropinquaverunt
castello quo ibant: et ipse se finxit
longius ire. Lucas 24:13,15,28

Et coegerunt illum, dicentes: Mane nobiscum, quoniam
advesperascit, et inclinata est jam
dies. Et intravit cum illis.
Lucas 24:29

Et factum est, dum recumberet cum eis, accepit
panem, et benedixit, ac fregit, et porrigebat
illis. Et aperti sunt oculi eorum, et cognoverunt
eum: et ipse evanuit ex oculis eorum.
Lucas 24:30,31

... Two of them went ... to a town ... named Emmaus. ... Jesus himself also, drawing near, went with them. ... And they drew nigh to the town whither they were going: and he made as though he would go farther. Luke 24:13,15,28

But they constrained him, saying: Stay with us, because it is towards evening and the day is now far spent. And he went in with them.

Luke 24:29

When he was at table with them, he took the bread and blessed, and broke it, and gave it to them. And their eyes were opened and they recognized him; and he vanished out of their sight.

Luke 24:30,31

Gloria Patri, et Filio, et Spiritui Sancto. Sicut
erat in principio, et nunc, et
semper, et in saecula
saeculorum.
Amen.

O mi Jesu, dimitte nobis debita nostra, libera
nos ab igne inferni, conduc in caelum
omnes animas, praesertim
illas, quae maxime indigent
misericordia Tua.

Glory be to the Father, and to the Son, and
to the Holy Spirit. As it was in the
beginning, is now, and ever
shall be. World without
end. Amen.

O my Jesus, forgive us our sins, save us from
the fires of hell. Lead all souls to heaven
especially those who are most
in need of Thy
mercy.

The Immaculate Conception
Giovanni Battista Tiepolo (1696 - 1770)

"...in the end my Immaculate Heart
will triumph."

—Our Lady of Fatima, July 13, 1917

Saint Joseph and Jesus with
John the Baptist
Melchior Paul von Deschwanden (1811 - 1881)

The Special Graces
Accorded Saint Joseph

This is the general rule that applies to all individual graces given to a rational creature. Whenever divine grace selects someone to receive a particular grace, or some especially favoured position, all the gifts for his state are given to that person, and enrich him abundantly.

This is especially true of that holy man Joseph, the supposed father of our Lord Jesus Christ, and true husband of the queen of the world and of the angels. He was chosen by the eternal Father to be the faithful foster-parent and guardian of the most precious treasures of God, his Son and his Spouse. This was the task which he so faithfully carried out. For this, the Lord said to him, "Good and faithful servant, enter into the joy of your Lord."

—Saint Bernardine of Siena (1380 - 1444)

Index of Meditations

Page

Bernard De Chartres
We Stand on the Shoulders of Giants 25
John of Salisbury: *The Metalogicon* 1159
Public Domain

Blessed Jacopone da Todi
Seeking Jesus
The Lauds 95
© Paulist Press. Used with permission.

Blessed Pope Paul VI
The Sacrament of Marriage 239
"Humanae Vitae", July 25, 1968
© Libreria Editrice Vaticana.
Used with permission.

James Burke
Illuminated Manuscripts Quote 17
The Day the Universe Changed
©1985 by London Writers Ltd.
Used by permission of Little, Brown and Co.

Pope Benedict XVI
The Baptism of Jesus 227
*Jesus of Nazareth: From the Baptism in the
Jordan to the Transfiguration*
© Libreria Editrice Vaticana.
Used with permission.

Pope Francis
The Cross Contains all the Love of God 149
"Way of the Cross with the Young
People Address"
World Youth Day XXVIII, Rio De Janeiro
© Libreria Editrice Vaticana.
Used with permission.

Pope Saint John XXIII
Latin as the Language of the Church 10
Apostolic Constitution "Veterum Sapientia"
© Libreria Editrice Vaticana.
Used with permission.

Pope Saint John Paul II
The Eucharist — The Source and
Summit of the Christian Life 277
"Ecclesia de Eucharistia", 2004
© Libreria Editrice Vaticana.
Used with permission.

Pope Saint Leo the Great
The Divinity of Jesus Made Manifest
to His Chosen Apostles 263
Sermon #51
© Libreria Editrice Vaticana.
Used with permission.

Pope Saint Pius X
The Assumption of the Virgin Mary 203
"Prayer to Our Lady of the Assumption"
© Libreria Editrice Vaticana.
Used with permission.

Saint Athanasius of Alexandria
Mary, the Ark of the New Covenant 51
Homily of the Papyrus of Turin 71:216
© Ignatius Press. Used with permission.

Saint Augustine
The Perpetual Virginity of Mary 75
Summa Theologica, III.Q.28, Objection 6
St. Thomas Aquinas quoting St. Augustine
newadvent.org. Used with permission.

Saint Bernardine of Siena
The Graces Granted to Saint Joseph 297
Sermon 2, "On Saint Joseph"
© Libreria Editrice Vaticana.
Used with permission.

Saint Bonaventure
Perfect Charity 61
The Perfect Love of God
Herder Book Company
Public Domain

Saint Francis of Assisi
Perfect Obedience 85
Saint Francis of Assisi: A Biography
by Johannes Jorgensen
© Doubleday Image Books.
Used with permission.

Saint John Chrysostom
Whose Sins You Shall Forgive
are Forgiven Them 165
St. John Chrysostom: *Six Books on the Priesthood*, Book 3.5
© Saint Vladimir's Press.
Used with permission.

Saint John Houghton
The Virtue of Courage 129
The London Charterhouse: Its Monks and Martyrs by Dom Laurence Hendriks
Kegan Paul, Trench & Co., London 1889
Public domain

Saint Louis De Montfort
Mary, Queen of Heaven 215
True Devotion to Mary
The Fruits of the Hail Mary 9
True Devotion to Mary
© Montfort Publications.
Used with permission.

Saint (Maria) Faustina Kowalska
Divine Mercy 109
Diary of St. Maria Faustina Kowalska:
Divine Mercy in My Soul #1485
© Marian Fathers of the Immaculate
Conception of the B.V.M. All rights reserved.
Used with permission.

Servant of God Louis M. Martinez
The Two Necessary Sanctifiers 191
The Sanctifier
Public Domain

Frank Sheed
The Barque of Peter 251
Theology and Sanity
© Ignatius Press. Used with permission.

Thomas à Kempis
Self-Denial 119
The Imitation of Christ, Book 3, #32
The Fewness of Those Who Love the
Cross of Jesus 139
The Imitation of Christ, Book 2, #11
© Ignatius Press. Used with permission.

Venerable Fulton J. Sheen
The Rosary 8
The World's First Love: Mary Mother of God.
The Virtue of Hope 179
Excerpts from his February 18, 1940 address
Permission to use the reflections of Fulton J.
Sheen was granted by "The Estate of Fulton J.
Sheen/The Society for the Propagation of the
Faith."/www.missio.org.

Index of Sacred Art

Page

Blessed Fra Angelico
The Annunciation 50

Cornelis de Baellieur
Adoration of the Child 74

William-Adolphe Bouguereau
Virgin and Child 20
Courtesy of Restored Traditions

The Flagellation of Christ 118

Annibale Carracci
The Baptism of Christ 226

Ludovico Carracci
The Presentation in the Temple 84

Sebastiano Conca
Christ in the Garden of Gethsemane 108

Correggio
Noli Me Tangere 164

Melchior Paul von Deschwanden
St. Joseph and Jesus with John the
Baptist 296
Photo courtesy of Wolfgang Moroder

Juan de Flandes
The Marriage Feast at Cana 238

Master of the Salem Heiligenaltar
The Pentecost 190

Maarten van Heemskerk
The Crowning with Thorns 128

Heinrich Hofmann
Christ in the Temple at Twelve 94

Page

Lorenzo Lotto
Christ Carrying the Cross 138

Master M. S.
The Visitation 60

Pietro Perugino
The Transfiguration 262

Sano di Pietro
Assumption of the Virgin 202

Rembrandt
The Storm on the Sea of Galilee 250

Peter Paul Rubens
The Elevation of the Cross 148

Giovanni Battista Tiepolo
The Immaculate Conception 294

Page

Titian
The Supper at Emmaus 276

Hubert and Jan Van Eyck
The Queenship of the Virgin Mary 214

Benjamin West
The Ascension of Christ 178

Consummatum Est.

It is Consummated.